THE NOTARY SOLUTION

Create a profitable first-class legal practice that allows time-freedom and career flexibility

KATHERINE BECKETT

R^ethink

First published in Great Britain in 2024
by Rethink Press (www.rethinkpress.com)

Contents

Introduction

Your notarial faculty is your magic wand. However, for notary publics practising in England and Wales, it can often feel like a double-edged sword.

I am the founder and owner of The Notary Solution. I have worked as a solicitor-notary and as a sole practitioner notary. I have practised from offices within law firms and I have seen clients at my home. I have built up a six-figure practice while raising two children. I have started from scratch in different locations, including London, Newcastle and Leeds, to build new notarial practices and have worked closely with other notaries to help them to build their own ideal practices, both as solicitor-notaries and as sole practitioners.

Practising as a notary public and working with hundreds of other notaries over the last twenty years, I have seen first-hand the conflict, hardship and headaches that a notarial qualification can cause for solicitor-notaries as they try to juggle their workload while dealing with stressed-out notarial clients who need urgent attention and assistance with documents that are unfamiliar and foreign. I have witnessed sole practitioner notaries battle to balance their time and attention and to create a profitable practice that is reliable and enjoyable to run. Without the necessary tools in place, a notarial practice can quickly become inefficient, unprofitable and cumbersome to manage.

I wrote this book to help both newly qualified and established notaries in England and Wales develop their own notarial practices into businesses that they love and can enjoy running for a long time. I know that any notary at any stage in their career can build a first-class notarial practice. Through coaching and training, I have seen individuals turbo-charge their enthusiasm for their practices and reignite their passion for delivering high-quality notarial services. I have witnessed notaries skyrocket in confidence as they take back control of their businesses and redesign their practices into profit-generating machines that are a pleasure to manage and develop.

I want you to do excellent work for your clients and to see the alchemy in the notarial qualification that you worked so hard to obtain. I want you to gain time-freedom and career flexibility while generating abundant profit and I am confident that you can create opportunities for yourself to build your ideal client base as both a notary and a solicitor.

The Notary Solution method

The Notary Solution will give you the tools to be able to integrate your notarial practice into your legal career and harmonise it with the rest of your life. It consists of three key steps, as follows:

1. Design your practice

2. Apply the pillars of notarial practice

3. Build your business

To create a first-class notarial practice that generates abundant profit, time-freedom and career flexibility, you must first design your ideal practice. This means that you consciously decide who you serve, where you work and how you operate. Then you must apply the pillars of notarial practice – being visible, expert, efficient and bold – to create your dream notarial practice and build a successful business.

- Be **visible**: You must be willing to stand out from the crowd and wear your notarial hat with pride and purpose. Let the right people know who you are, what you know and what you can do for them.

- Be **expert**: An expert notary public requires an excellent attitude to change and learning – you must commit to being at the cutting edge of the profession. You cannot run a first-class practice unless you want to become an expert at the work you do.

- Be **efficient**: Your notarial practice must be efficient at every level. There are many barriers to efficiency, but essentially it relates to what you are willing to do and what you are willing to stop doing.

- Be **bold**: You must be fearless in making your ideal notarial practice a reality. Building a successful notarial practice is not for the fainthearted. The work required is going to challenge you and make you uncomfortable on a regular basis, even if you are a well-established notary public.

Finally, you must build the business you've designed. We'll talk about how to do this in Part Three. This requires you to go beyond the theoretical and the good intentions, formulate a personalised game plan that you follow consistently, and be disciplined in taking the action steps required. In this part, we will also discuss how our practices fit into the larger legal system and what we must do as individuals to contribute to this wonderful profession and ensure that it endures into the next century and beyond.

My promise to you is that once you have read this book and taken the actions required, you will realise the untapped value of your notarial faculty and be able to open up a new world of possibilities and potential. You will remember why you qualified as a notary and how proud you were when you did. You will have a game plan to release the magic of your qualification with ease and enthusiasm.

Throughout the book, I use hypothetical case studies to demonstrate the teaching points. These are fictional notaries but if you see yourself in them, this is intentional. Let us begin...

PART ONE
DESIGN YOUR PRACTICE

W hen used correctly, your status as a notary is a master key. It can be used to open doors that would otherwise be shut to you. For solicitor-notaries, it is the most elegant networking tool you will ever have or need, a way to meet potential new clients in a business setting without even setting foot outside your practice. For sole practitioners, it is the access code that enables you to create an abundant business that you can run around the rest of your life and family. To make the best use of this key and open as many doors as possible, you need to design an ideal practice that will work for you and your clients.

Your notarial practice must have longevity, which means that it needs to be curated for you. Only you know what would suit you best. You are a notary public but you are not a public service. You want to design your practice to work in harmony with the rest of your life, including your solicitor practice if you have one, or any other work that you do. You should also consider your family setup, your location and your expertise. You must decide who you will serve, how you will deliver services and when you will do so.

This is the blueprint that you are working towards. Once you know where you want to go, you can start unlocking the way forward.

ONE
Who

A this stage, you are designing your ideal notarial practice, one that you will enjoy running for many years. In doing so, it is useful to think of your hypothetical ideal clients so that you can develop a blueprint of a practice that provides a solution tailored to them. This is the 'who' part of your vision. The purpose of designing your ideal client base is to give your business focus and intentionality, something to work toward.

The Notaries Practice Rules[1] make it clear that a notary must act impartially and provide a prompt and proper standard of care to all clients. However,

---

1 The Faculty Office, *Notaries Practice Rules* (2019), www.facultyoffice. org.uk/wp-content/uploads/2023/10/Notaries-Practice-Rules-2019. pdf, accessed November 2023

this does not mean that you cannot design your ideal client base. It means that you cannot refuse to act for clients for anything other than a legitimate reason. If you have not read the Practice Rules recently, make this your first task.

It is a mistake for notaries to think that they cannot influence their client base. Provided that you are compliant with the Faculty Office rules and regulations, it is sound business to ensure that you are making yourself known to the people and businesses that you are best placed to serve. You are a public officer, which means that you are offering a service to the public – it doesn't mean that you can or must serve all people at all times.

You cannot market effectively to 'everyone who needs a notary' or build a first-class practice on the assumption that everyone who needs a notary will find you. You need to decide on your ideal client mix, location and niche, and then design (or redesign) your practice around this. Consciously choosing who you are best placed to serve and the client mix that is most advantageous to your practice does not mean that you should turn clients away. I run a predominantly commercial practice, but I advise a great deal of individual clients too. I provide information and assistance, and sometimes this means redirecting enquirers to other solutions – even other notaries – that will be better suited to them.

Client mix

Visualise a day of seeing clients and drafting documents. What percentage of your client base do you
want to be commercial? If you are a solicitor-notary,
does your solicitor work afford you sufficient flexibility to service commercial clients as a notary? If you
are a litigator or family law specialist, for example,
who needs to commit to court dates at short notice,
you may find that working for a busy commercial client would create an unhelpful conflict between your
two businesses.

Based on my experience, to have a successful notarial
practice it is best to have some commercial clients, but
you must be honest about the commercial clients that
you want. Often, we can be driven by ego, deciding
that we want to work for the top commercial clients
in our area. However, you need to consider the prac-
ticalities. Some companies require regular but routine
notarial services, such as pharmaceutical companies
needing assistance with regulatory paperwork. They
need a notary who is diligent and organised. Other
commercial clients are more high energy and require
a notary who can react quickly to urgent instructions
and be available at the exact moment that their managing director has a window in their schedule.

Remember, we are not talking about turning clients
away. We are designing your perfect practice with
a particular client base in mind, one that suits you.

Many notaries fear that in specifying which clients they are best placed to serve, they are somehow alienating others. At this stage, you are simply designing your ideal notarial practice and identifying the clients that would be most suited to that practice.

If your solicitor firm deals with mainly individual clients, it may suit you better to have mostly private clients as a notary. Or you might prefer a more relaxed way of working, one that does not require you to leave your office, and you could enjoy the variety that working with individual private clients allows. It's OK to want what you want. This is *your* practice.

Most notaries would like a healthy mix of commercial and private clients. That might not be a 50:50 split – you will know what would work best for you, taking into account your locality, your solicitor specialism and the work that you and your colleagues do. For example, if you work in the heart of a commercial district, it makes sense for your commercial client percentage to be higher.

CASE STUDY: Sarah

Sarah is a probate solicitor and a director in her well-established high-street practice. Based in the centre of town, her firm has great footfall and her marketing strategy as a solicitor is to target medium- to high-net-worth individuals. Her law firm prides itself on being inclusive, and the local network is hugely important to the business. As a notary, her ideal client base is the same as her solicitor client base. It is mainly private clients and local businesses who are happy to come to her office. She does not want to be on call for national commercial clients. She lives in town with her family and is happy working as a solicitor. She has no ambitions to become a sole practitioner notary. She has two administrative assistants who are keen to be trained up to be part of the notarial team and all her fees go to her law firm. Her ideal client mix is 80% private clients, and 20% commercial, with the commercial clients being comprised of local businesses.

Client location

You must also decide where your ideal clients are located. There is no benefit to making your life more difficult than it needs to be by targeting, for example, a big commercial client that frequently needs you to attend their office located 60 miles away, if this is not the best use of your time. Let your practice be easy.

If you enjoy being out and about, you can design a client base with a large radius. If you work from more than one location as a solicitor, you can factor this into your practice design. However, if you work all day in your office, just nipping out for a sandwich at lunchtime, you need your clients to be local to you and to be willing to come to your office. If you run (or want to run) a full-time notarial practice, you can consider national and even international clients.

It is sensible to consider the other notarial services that are currently available in your locality and who they are serving. It may be that there is a glut of notaries in one town but a void in a nearby area, and it can be simple and easy to set up in another location using a serviced office, for example. Analyse the types of businesses that exist around you and see whether you could position yourself conveniently for businesses that are likely to require notarial services.

CASE STUDY: Richard

Richard is a commercial property solicitor whose firm works exclusively with commercial clients. He is located in a large business park with little public transport access. While he is happy to provide a generic notarial service, he is best placed to deal with large commercial clients because he is used to dealing with directors and is especially comfortable with commercial law and the execution of commercial documents. As a commercial solicitor, he does not have a great deal of time available for his notarial work. His fees as a solicitor are high and for his notarial practice to be viable, his notarial fees need to be equivalent. With the right level of marketing, he has enough work available from his firm's commercial clients and the companies within a 10-mile radius to create a profitable and solid practice that he can continue to run effectively as a sole practitioner notary if he chooses to. His ideal client mix is 80% commercial clients, and 20% private clients, with the private clients most likely comprised of company directors and professionals.

WHO

Client niche

When designing your practice, you need to decide the type of client that is most suited to you and who you can best serve. The purpose of this is to create an ideal client avatar, which will guide your marketing and give you a focus when you are making business decisions. There are around 800 notaries in England and Wales – it would be a mistake to think that we should all run our practices in the same way. This would not be beneficial to the individual notaries or the profession. In identifying the type of clients that you most like to work with, you will be able to adapt your practice to this specific market, while maintaining your duty as a public official. The type of clients that you identify now as who you expect to be working with is your current best guess at how you will build your ideal notarial practice. This will change and evolve. Start where you are, with the information that you have available. Over time, you will find your client niche.

Establishing an area of expertise

Is there a particular source of work that is available to you, that it would make sense for you to become especially familiar with? At different times throughout my notarial career, I have targeted specific types of work, such as applications by medical practitioners to work in Australia, Indian powers of attorney, OCI affidavits and attestation of degree certificates for the

15

United Arab Emirates and China. My current client pool requires lots of powers of attorney for Spain, so I have made it my business to know as much as I can about this particular document. I am also well placed for dealing with commercial documents and I expect to be the go-to notary in my area for all commercial enquiries.

Identifying an area of expertise is a great way of establishing yourself within your client niche. Is there an obvious area of work that you can focus on in designing your ideal practice? This does not mean that you are eliminating other areas – not at all. It just means that you are noticing an opportunity to serve a particular niche and building this into your practice planning. For example, if you have a specific 'ex-pat' community within your locality, it could be logical to delve a little deeper into the knowledge you would need to assist with their notarial requirements and make yourself known to them. If you have a particular skill or specialism as a solicitor, does this put you in a better position to be able to act for a particular group of clients or to undertake specific instructions? It is also important to ask yourself if you enjoy that type of work – just because you can specialise in a specific area, does not mean that you must.

Once you have established your area of expertise and / or your niche, you need to make sure your potential clients know about it.

Developing your reputation

Building a reputation in your client niche takes effort. I cannot just decide that this is the work I want and do nothing to earn my reputation as the go-to notary for that particular instruction. However, the effort that it requires is not too arduous given the benefit. For example, if you want to be the primary notary in your area for dealing with degree certificates and criminal record checks, you must develop an excellent system for this type of work. You will need to know how to verify authenticity and become familiar with the requirements for the most frequently used embassies. You should encourage your clients to recommend you to their friends and contacts needing the same service and you must be prepared to work through the thorny issues that would potentially unhinge other notaries who are not willing to invest the time to understand them. You could quickly find that other notaries in the area do not want to spend their time dealing with these potentially long-winded enquiries and will happily refer them to you. Now you are building momentum and you are in a position to write helpful articles and social media posts on the subject, establishing your expertise.

CASE STUDY: Esther

Esther is head of the private client department for a large commercial law firm. Her ideal clients are professionals. She is extremely busy as a solicitor and does not have a great deal of time to devote to her notarial practice. She prefers it when her clients can give her clear instructions and can easily understand her explanations. She enjoys being a notary, especially being able to assist in more complex cases involving cross-jurisdictional Court of Protection issues, which is her specialism as a solicitor. Because of her high fee targets as a solicitor, she is probably the most expensive notary in her area. It would be pointless to market to all people requiring notarial services as she would not be the best option for everyone. She is best placed to assist existing clients of her law firm and high-net-worth individuals who can easily afford her fee and appreciate the level of expertise that she has.

She does not want to exclude anyone from access to her notarial services but wants to design her marketing and practice structure to appeal to those clients whom she is most suitable for.

Summary

When designing your ideal notarial practice, the first thing you should be thinking about is who you will be serving. When you know who you will be building your practice around – including the type of clients (commercial or private) you will mostly be serving, where they are located and what kind of work you'll be doing for them – it is easier to fill in the detail of your practice blueprint.

This will influence all the other decisions you make about how to best build your ideal business, so it's important to think about who you want to work with and what you will enjoy doing. You will be establishing an area of expertise and building a reputation based on the client mix and niche that you choose now, so take time to think about what an ideal practice looks like for you in terms of your ideal client base; then you can design a practice that works for you and for them.

ACTIONS

Ask yourself:

1. What is your ideal mix of commercial and private clients?
2. Are there any specific types of clients you are best placed to serve?
3. What geographical area can you cover?
4. Do you have a specialism or niche that you could develop as a notary?
5. Will you enjoy running a notarial practice with these clients?

TWO
How

To build a first-class notarial practice, you must consider the type of practice that you want to run. In this section, you are going to decide 'how' you will conduct your business, how you will define your style as a notary and how you will serve your clients. Even if you are an experienced notary public, you will be starting with a clean slate and designing a practice based on all the knowledge and experience you have accumulated.

Most notaries dive into their notarial practice without consciously deciding how they will conduct themselves as a notary public. Solicitor-notaries may start off working with another notary and simply emulate that notary's style. It seems logical to continue what we have been taught, but this is where we pick up most of our bad habits. When we first qualify, it is natural to charge what the other notaries are charging and try to make our documents look like their documents. However, as you are engineering a first-class practice that generates abundant profit, time-freedom and career flexibility, you must decide for yourself how you will manage your practice, taking into account your unique circumstances and preferences. This will create the best service for your clients too.

Fees

It doesn't matter what you charge or how you charge. It matters only whether your fee system works for you and your clients. You can charge on a time basis or a fixed-fee basis; both have their advantages.

Transparency

Transparency regarding fees is key. One of the biggest barriers to running a successful notarial practice is incongruences in beliefs about fees. This presents itself in a variety of ways. For example, some notaries are reluctant to be upfront and definite about fees. As a solicitor, you will have your hourly rate set in advance and in quoting for a matter, you will be required to state how long you expect it will take and either give an estimate of fees or a fixed fee (though usually with caveats to cover anything unexpected). As a notary, this approach does not work. Notarial instructions are relatively short and definite and you will have far more knowledge than the client regarding how long something will take and what is required. Solicitor-notaries that have been institutionalised into using six-minute units have forgotten that this is an accounting tool and not relevant to the end user. You must be confident in your knowledge and experience and provide transparent fee information. Occasionally, something will take longer than anticipated and, if you are working on a fixed fee, you should call this a learning experience and possibly adjust your fee rate going forwards. If this is happening frequently, you need to review your fees in general.

Some notaries appear defensive about fees. Many clients think that they just need a signature on a form. You do not need to take this personally. Try to see it from the client's point of view – understandably, they think this is all that is required. You should state your fee in a definite, confident and unapologetic manner and be able to explain the work involved, in a professional way, if the client needs this additional information. They rarely do. Often, over-explaining fees is just a bad habit that the notary has developed.

Sometimes the notary is unduly concerned about the competition and what other notaries are charging. You are in the process of designing and building a first-class notarial practice and you cannot run it in isolation. You will benefit from having other notaries in your area and do not need to be secretive about what you're charging or paranoid about them taking your clients. As a first-class notary, you must be confident enough in your practice to be able to out-class any competition and to be able to work effectively with other notaries to mutually benefit both practices.

Price list

A good way to ensure transparency is to have a set price list. Now and then, a notary decides what to charge based on what they think the client can or will pay. This guessing game is a disastrous approach and one that many notaries don't even realise that they are using. It is unfair to your client base as a whole to adjust your fee based on what you think a client expects to pay. In exceptional circumstances, you can waive or reduce your fee, but you should be able to provide a legitimate reason for doing so, and not just because you felt sorry for the client that day. This is not to squeeze every penny out of every client but to create trust around your practice. I find that a written price list for doing fee quotes is the best way to achieve this kind of transparency.

A price list will also enable you to effectively delegate quoting tasks. Having a simple and robust fee structure and adequate support systems in place will help to ensure that you are running an efficient and profitable business in conjunction with your other legal work.

CASE STUDY: Jonathan

Jonathan is a sole practitioner notary in London. He has a small office, but he considers himself to be mobile and this is his USP with commercial clients. He knows London well and is happy to cover a large area. Jonathan must take account of the travel time in his fee quotes to be profitable. His commercial clients prefer him to charge fixed fees, but they do not need him to explain his rates. For this reason, Jonathan includes a set travel time in his notarial rate and his clients are happy with this. Jonathan charges a premium commercial rate that reflects how valuable his service is to his clients. His flexibility means that he is available at his clients' offices when they need him, and this warrants a high fee that his clients are willing to pay. In designing the mechanics of his notarial practice, Jonathan works from a simple price list that his clients can rely on and he keeps his overheads low to ensure a healthy profit.

Retaining notarial income as a solicitor

One problem that I see regularly is a notary keeping notarial fees separate from their solicitor business and then retaining the notarial fees. This creates unnecessary stress and tension for solicitor-notaries because it makes them 'squirrelly' about their notary work, which is the exact opposite of what is required for a successful notarial practice. Your solicitor colleagues need to understand and celebrate your notary work and see all the ways that it benefits your firm as a whole. There is nothing that will create a quicker and

25

more entrenched distrust than seeing a colleague lining his pocket, which is often what it feels like when a solicitor-notary keeps their notarial fees separate, regardless of all the other benefits they are bringing to the firm. If this is your current fee arrangement, keep an open mind about the benefits of changing this.

CASE STUDY: Amanda

Amanda is a solicitor-notary with two legal assistants. She has taken the time to create a price list for the notarial work and empowered her assistants to give fee quotes to notarial clients. This required her to train them initially, but she has found that this was time well spent as she does not need to review every notary enquiry personally. What seemed like a difficult task at first, turned out to be quite simple once she committed to putting her fees in writing. Her assistants know to refer any particularly complex enquiries to her but 90% of the time, the fee quotes are routine. This saves her a huge amount of time, not just in terms of creating the fee quotes but also because she does not get involved in any discussions regarding those fees.

Business structure

Notaries can make running a practice so much harder than it needs to be. I've been guilty of this myself. In terms of business model, it is simple – don't overcomplicate it. Build ease into the structure. I think that the root cause of overly complex structures relates to the flawed premise that notaries have to justify their fees. We don't want things to look too simple like we are 'just stamping documents'. Sometimes, though, it's just that we haven't taken the time to stand back and evaluate how we can make things easier.

Running your practice can be as easy or as difficult as you are willing to tolerate. There is always an easier way to do things. Imagine that you are dealing with ten times the number of documents that you are currently, how would you do things differently? Which tasks would you delegate and who would you need help from to ensure everything functioned with ease? If you are a solicitor-notary, notarial practice should be considered a department in its own right. There may only be one notary but the department is a team effort; it is a hybrid, somewhere between a marketing department and a fee-earning department. It is much more valuable than simply the fees it generates. Even if you are a sole practitioner, don't assume that you have to take care of every aspect of your practice personally. The ability to delegate effectively is a skill that has to be practised and perfected.

To achieve this, you must build a notarial team with the resources that you have available and ensure that your workspace is functional and a pleasurable place to work from.

Your team

You do not need to do everything yourself, and you will be more profitable when you do not attempt to. Over the years, I have tried many different ways to be more efficient by delegating tasks within the practice. Some of these have worked and some have not. I tried using a phone answering service which I thought was going to be a game changer, but I quickly realised that this added a layer of complexity without relieving any pressure. I also tried to delegate the social media function but found that it worked better when I was managing this myself as the posts and comments were more authentic.

In designing your ideal notarial practice, you need to decide the level of support you want in your business. Your team will encompass both staff and suppliers – that means any colleagues, a legalisation agent, stationer, IT consultant, administrative assistants and all manner of people that are not in your direct employment. When assessing your current supplier and staff requirements, there will be obvious gaps that you can easily address. Where have you overcomplicated your practice? Is there anyone involved that does not make things better?

It may be that you do not have the personnel available immediately, but this does not mean that you cannot design your ideal infrastructure. It just means that you may have to take more of the roles yourself until you can demonstrate the integrity of the system to your colleagues, or you can hire someone to join you. Remember, it does not necessarily need to be someone in the same room as you or even the same country. Technology can facilitate seamless remote working. They don't have to be a full-time member of staff or someone within your direct employment. Be open minded about the options available to you. The how is not as important as the why.

Many solicitor-notaries have a marketing professional at their firm who can breathe life into a notarial marketing campaign and an IT consultant who can revamp a LinkedIn profile in less than an hour. If you had some postcards printed, is there an office junior you could task with delivering a handful to each of the law firms in town? Is there an associate who could systematically look at your diary and offer a helpful legal review to each notary client after their appointment? Could you train an assistant to take charge of the legalisation process, including the follow-up once the attestation is complete? Solicitor-notaries have a phenomenal team of accomplished professionals available if they would only take the time to involve them in the notarial practice. Sole practitioner notaries will also potentially have an array of helpful team members that they could delegate to, even if it means asking a family member to take on the task of going to the Post Office or managing bookkeeping or social media. This is not because you cannot do things yourself, but because it will make your business run more smoothly to delegate these tasks.

CASE STUDY: Charles

Charles has always run his notarial practice himself, dealing with all aspects of the work from speaking to the clients, drafting the documents, dealing with legalisation and invoicing. He found this was the easiest way to keep on track with everything. However, as his solicitor and notarial practices have grown and evolved, he would love to be able to delegate some aspects of the notarial practice but cannot find the time to train someone or make the necessary changes.

First, Charles needs to accept that many aspects of his notarial practice can be delegated. The easiest place to start is to work out what must be done by the notary personally. Then he can identify what resources he has access to that could assist him. A systematic approach is needed to put together his notarial team and work out what training is required.

In my experience, people vastly overestimate the complexity of their practices and, once they are willing to relinquish some control, they are pleasantly surprised by the efficiency that the routine nature of the work allows.

Location

You are designing your ideal notarial practice that is going to grow with you and serve you for years to come. Where would you most like to work? If your law firm has more than one office, but it is not convenient for you to work from a particular location, you do not have to advertise notarial services as being available there. If you could shift your location to somewhere particularly appealing to you, where would that be? Do you think that this would be useful to clients too? If you want to work from home, can you imagine clients coming into your workspace?

If you don't have the perfect workspace right now, don't let this deter you from starting to create your ideal notarial practice. It is a mistake to think that you must have the perfect space to see clients; often, they do not care, provided that they get their documents notarised. In analysing your location, you are planning your perfect practice, both now and in the future. There may be two different versions of your ideal practice that you can work on simultaneously.

Your workspace

Imagine your ideal workspace. Do you picture a pristine, Scandinavian-style clinic? A glass-fronted city office? Or an elegant study with period features and a big wooden desk? This is your perfect practice, so there is no incorrect answer. You can build your practice to look however you want it to. Would you prefer a purpose-built soundproof pod in your garden or a serviced office with parking?

You may already be committed to a particular location but there is always an element of control over deciding where you will see notarial clients and this should tie in perfectly with the way that you want to work as a solicitor. For example, you may want to set up a particular meeting room where you see your notarial clients, one that has a scanner paired with your laptop and your notarial stationery box locked away, that is easily accessed from reception. Your first-class notarial practice must have 'ease' woven into its very fabric so that it is a pleasure to own and manage and, as it evolves, it grows easily and organically without becoming unwieldy and burdensome.

CASE STUDY: Robert

Robert lives in a rural location in a small commuter town between two large commercial cities. He would love to work from home and has a bright and pleasant office in the extension at the back of his house with its own access door. His children are grown up and he lives with his wife, who works three days a week. He would like to run a thriving notarial practice but does not believe there would be sufficient work locally. There is a train station at the end of his road with direct routes to both city centres, each thirty minutes away. He decides that his ideal location would be to work from an office in each city one day a week and from home one day a week. He rents a virtual office with a meeting space in each city location and devises his marketing campaign accordingly.

Summary

How you run your practice is your choice. As a solicitor-notary, your notarial practice should complement and enhance your solicitor practice. It should never conflict with your solicitor work and this takes conscious planning.

One of the first things you need to consider in how you'll run your practice is how and what you'll charge. Ensuring your practice is profitable is key to making it a success as either a freestanding business or a department of your law firm. You also need to think about how your business will be structured, what support you will have access to and who you will be working with. Your location will be a big factor in how you run your business, so you need to decide where you will be working from, how mobile you want to be and what your workspace needs to be equipped with for you to run your practice with ease.

ACTIONS

Think about:

1. How would you define your notarial style?
2. How would you operate your ideal notarial practice?
3. Are you happy with your current fee system?
4. Where is your ideal notarial practice located?
5. What would your ideal notarial workspace look like? Describe it.

THREE
When

In designing your ideal notarial practice, you must decide when you will see clients, when you will deal with enquiries, how much time you will spend with each client and how long you are willing to spend travelling. As a first-class notary, you must be in charge of your schedule.

If you are a solicitor-notary, you must compartmentalise your notarial work so that it can co-exist in harmony with your solicitor work. You cannot properly use your notarial faculty to create career flexibility if your solicitor work is suffering, even superficially, because of your notarial practice. This means that you must be excelling as a solicitor, exceeding all your targets and doing everything that is required of you. Your notarial practice should be an asset to you and your firm.

If you are a sole practitioner notary, it can be tempting to say yes to every client and ask when is best for them. If this works for you, then it's not a problem, but often the lack of firm boundaries between appointment times and the rest of life creates unnecessary noise and logistical tension that is difficult to switch off. I know that it is tempting to adjust your timetable to make yourself available for every instruction to avoid missing out, but the fear that drives this behaviour is rooted in a scarcity mindset. Sometimes, it is because we are overly empathetic and want to help the client. Mostly, it is a bad habit and a lack of planning.

Notarial work is fast and each matter is relatively short. We get a dopamine hit every time we take a phone call or respond to an email. As a species, humans are task-orientated and get satisfaction from completing things. I still enjoy checking the post box and opening envelopes. I like to put the documents into neat little piles. This is a ridiculous waste of my time but I enjoy it all the same. In general, our notary work is easier and quicker than our solicitor work. If the action carries with it the promise of cash in the bank, it is difficult to resist. If that money is going to come to you personally, of course, you are going to deal with it. This is why it is vital to be honest with yourself about when and how you will do things.

Scheduling

A mistake that so many notaries make is that we allow clients and potential clients to decide how we will manage our time, which makes us stressed and unproductive. If you're going to design a practice with scalability and longevity, it is essential to build into your schedule when you will be available to assist clients with enquiries, respond to emails, attend appointments and notarise documents.

In designing your perfect notarial practice, you must assess when you will see clients and for how long. In addition, you will need to factor in when you will respond to notarial enquiries and prepare documents, deal with invoices and payments and legalisation requirements. This is not a difficult task. You are well able, I am sure, to look at your calendar and mark out appropriate blocks of time for each task. The harder part is being disciplined in sticking to this.

In deciding when you will see clients, you must strike a balance between what will work for you and what will work for clients. If you need thirty minutes to get into the office and deal with 'staff and stuff', don't arrange notary appointments for 9am. If you have an assistant, don't arrange appointments over lunch when your assistant will be unavailable. Make life as easy as possible for yourself, provided that it also works for clients.

Appointment length

Most notaries allocate too long for each appointment. This could be because your calendar system creates a thirty-minute meeting by default, or because you once needed thirty minutes to deal with each appointment and this standard has not been altered to reflect your experience and progression. Most often, it is because the notary has not allocated time to deal with the document in advance and has therefore built in extra time to deal with anything unexpected.

As I do not work as a solicitor and therefore do not need any time for cross-referral, I allocate twenty minutes per appointment and I schedule them back-to-back as though I am running a clinic. I allow two hours on a Tuesday and Thursday morning that my assistant can book without checking with me. I see commercial clients that want me to come to their offices on Tuesday and Thursday afternoons. I see most commercial clients in my office.

The more time I give myself for an appointment, the longer the appointment takes. When I am focused, I get the work done promptly. Short appointment times require you to be organised in advance and to have prepared the client for the meeting. It is your job to make sure that the meeting runs on time, that the client knows what to expect, where to come to and what to bring. There should be no surprises at the appointment. You should have read the documents in advance and dealt with any issues.

The way that you conduct yourself also determines whether the meeting is going to run on time or run away with you. From your first interaction with the client, you should establish that you are in charge of this aspect of the transaction. You must have authority with the client because this is your job as a notary. Your duty is to the transaction, so you must look beyond the individuals involved in the appointment and remember the people not in the room who will rely on the notarised document. This is not always easy, but you must establish this dynamic with the client from the outset.

Some common pitfalls can cause appointments to overrun. If you consider these in advance you can create a plan of action so that you are fully prepared. In my experience, the most frequent hiccups include:

- The client has not got the correct ID documents

- The client is late

- The client produces additional documents

- Language difficulties or a complication not previously mentioned

- You raise questions at the meeting that the client needs to check with a lawyer overseas

- IT malfunction

These issues will not trip you up if you have a clear policy in place. For example, if the client has not brought their passport, I will deal with the document as planned but retain the document until the client has returned with their passport. Because I have this solution determined in advance, it does not interrupt the flow of our meeting.

CASE STUDY: David

David is a solicitor-notary who enjoys his notary work but feels frustrated when the clients arrive without the correct identification and documentation. He feels that he is clear before the appointment, but this is something that happens regularly. He asks his trainee solicitor to review his appointment procedures and see where he could be clearer for clients. His trainee quickly identifies that he is putting too much information in his appointment confirmation email and is giving the client too many options, so the salient details are getting lost. She devises him a template email with bullet points for the client and direct instructions in bold. She attaches the invoice and terms of business as two separate documents and cuts down the email to a third of its original length. She also suggests sending a reminder email to the client on the morning of their appointment, stating: 'You must bring your passport and proof of address.' Using the template email, this process only takes his assistant a couple of minutes but it dramatically improves the efficiency of the notarial practice.

Availability

Traditionally, opening hours for a law firm would be 9am to 5pm, or somewhere in that region. Now, thanks to modern technology, notarial opening hours can be 6am until 11pm. Sometimes that is due to the client, but mostly it is down to the notary's weakly enforced boundaries and lack of structure.

Working all hours is an indication that we do not have the correct framework in place to run our notarial practice efficiently. We have not trained and empowered staff to deal with enquiries and to give fee quotes or deal with document preparation from precedents. We have not set specific client appointment times and we have not built in holidays in advance. Ultimately, it comes down to self-discipline and standards.

As a notary, you get to choose your opening hours. You are not the fourth emergency service and you do not need to be on call. You are designing a first-class notarial practice that suits you perfectly and works well for your clients. You need to consciously decide your opening hours and then you need to stick to them in the knowledge that this is the best thing for you, for your notarial practice and, therefore, for your clients too.

Clinic times

If you are a solicitor-notary, it is tempting to think that if you are in the office anyway you can see clients at any time. This does not show sufficient respect for your solicitor work. You cannot be a brilliant notary and an average solicitor. The two go hand in hand. To do otherwise is like heating a room but leaving the window open. You can build in flexibility but it works best to have specific times that you will see notary clients. You can decide when this will be, but to be available at any time is energy-draining and unnecessary.

For sole practitioner notaries, it is equally important that you are deliberate with your time and availability. You are designing a practice that you love. You do not have to be available sixteen hours a day. There may be a bit of trial and error that goes into this, but take charge of your schedule and see how that conserves your energy within your practice. I can guarantee that there will be an occasion when you miss out on an instruction but overall, this is how you build a robust and profitable practice. Clients will rearrange their day to fit in with your practice hours and this will enable you to maintain the energy that you need to complete all the other work required to build a first-class practice.

CASE STUDY: Harjit

Harjit is a solicitor-notary in a medium-sized law firm. She has been a notary for three years and has become used to the interruptions to her solicitor work from notarial enquiries, but wants to manage her work better. As an experiment, she decides that she will give herself fifteen minutes in the morning and afternoon to deal with notarial enquiries and ninety minutes on Wednesday and Friday mornings to see notary clients. This will allow her to see up to six clients a week. In addition, she is going to offer every client a free legal review from her law firm. It takes a great deal of discipline at first not to respond immediately to every notarial enquiry but she asks her receptionist to take a name, email and phone number and send her an email instead of putting the call through to her. She then puts the emails into a folder that she responds to at 9.30 or 16.30 every day. This simple shift changes the whole tone of her notarial practice. Notarial enquiries are dealt with swiftly and efficiently, clients are responded to quickly and decisions regarding appointments are made almost immediately.

Holidays and breaks

In addition to your working hours, you must build into your ideal practice the ability to take a holiday, and you should be able to schedule this in advance. It is not always easy, I know. I struggle to get this right myself, however, we are designing an ideal practice. You need to take regular breaks and so you need to have a system for being able to down tools.

Ideally, you should have an arrangement with another local notary to be able to cover each other's holiday and you should have systems in place to advise clients when you cannot assist with enquiries for some time. At the very least, you should have the technology and the tools to be able to take a break without it causing too much stress – whatever that looks like for you. I find it easier to step away from the office if I am contactable. I don't like to be entirely absent. I can relax more knowing that I will be called in an emergency, but will otherwise be unavailable for a week. Other notaries I know love to power off completely and set up an out-of-hours auto-responder on their phone and email.

Looking to the future

The point of designing your ideal notarial practice is to create something that will work for you long term. Many solicitor-notaries continue to run their notarial practice after they have retired as solicitors. I retired as a solicitor in my twenties and became a full-time notary. Career flexibility is one of the superpowers granted by your notarial faculty.

In designing your notarial practice blueprint, allow yourself to think long term and factor that into the plan. Try to see the whole picture; you should have an exit strategy in place from the beginning. Scalability means that your notarial practice can grow beyond what it is now without you having to redesign the whole business model. For your practice to be scalable, it should be able to manage twice as many documents without having an adverse impact. Your practice should have room to grow.

If you are unsure which direction you want to take it in, you need to incorporate options and flexibility into your practice. If you are a newly qualified notary and do not yet know what is possible, you can still plan your ideal practice but in more general terms. When you first start out, all experience is valuable. It is fine to accept any instruction that comes your way for the first six to twelve months, at which point you will have more information to play with. If you are a solicitor-notary, it is vital to discuss this policy with your head of department or partners so that you can check in regularly and ensure that your notary work is not having a detrimental impact on your solicitor work. Some sole practitioners opt to work a couple of days a week as a consultant solicitor while they build up their notarial practice.

CASE STUDY: John

John is an employment solicitor and qualified as a notary five years ago when the firm's notary was retiring. He enjoys the notary work but he has ambitions to become the managing partner at his law firm. He sees the value of the notarial service that he provides and would love another notary at his firm to qualify to take over the day-to-day practice. His ideal would be to have a brilliant notarial department within his law firm but to be able to share the workload with another lawyer. He has great ideas but lacks the time to execute them. John's notarial blueprint should involve another solicitor training as a notary and building a notarial team with the right marketing and admin support. He appreciates that it will take up to five years to be fully functional and is excited to get started.

Summary

This chapter has focused on the 'when' of your ideal practice. This is about what your days and weeks as a practising notary will look like – how many hours a week you'll spend with clients and on which days, when you will be available to deal with notarial enquiries, how long appointments will be and how much time you allocate to admin tasks. You also need to factor in holidays that you will take (remember, this is your *ideal* practice) and how you will facilitate this. Don't be afraid to tweak your plan to build in a safety net or transition plan.

If you're a solicitor-notary, you need to consider how you will balance your notarial and solicitor work. If you're a notary only, you must think about how you will balance your days. Notary work lends itself well to automation and time blocking, as it involves many repeated and similar tasks. A first-class notary will make use of all such tools to ensure they manage their time effectively.

ACTIONS

1. What are the ideal opening hours for your notarial practice?

2. What other factors must you consider in building your plan?

3. How long do you need for each appointment?

4. Does your blueprint work for you long term and is it scalable?

5. What is your exit strategy?

PART TWO
THE PILLARS

O nce you have decided the who, how and when of your practice, you need to figure out how you will make it work. This is where my pillars of notarial practice come in. To build a first-class notarial practice that generates abundant profit, time-freedom and career flexibility you must be **visible**, **expert**, **efficient** and **bold**. In the Notaries Practice Rules,[2] the Faculty Office sets the minimum standard at which you must operate, but this does not guarantee you success as a notary public.

Before you move on to the pillars of notarial practice, return to your practice blueprint and ensure it is

2   The Faculty Office, *Notaries Practice Rules* (2019), www.facultyoffice.
org.uk/wp-content/uploads/2023/10/Notaries-Practice-Rules-2019.
pdf, accessed November 2023

aspirational enough to get you motivated and ambitious enough to be something worth working towards.

When you have your ideal practice blueprint, you must continually review your performance in each of these four pillars and adjust as needed to make that ideal a reality. This is simple but not easy. Regardless of where you are in your notarial career, it will require a significant commitment from you and a willingness to expand beyond your current comfort zone.

FOUR

Be Visible

To build a successful practice, you must first be prepared to stand out from the crowd and wear your notarial hat with pride and purpose. Many people feel overwhelmed by the task of becoming more visible. You may not be comfortable with being photographed or on film. That's OK, you can work up to this. You don't have to take on celebrity status; you just have to be willing to let your light shine brightly. There are so many ways that you can do this. The most important thing is that you start.

To achieve visibility, you will need a personalised marketing strategy that you apply consistently to let everyone know who you are, what you know and what you can do for them. For many lawyers, this is unfamiliar territory. We are used to being team players and it can be alien and uncomfortable to shout about our individual knowledge and skills. As solicitors, we are trained to play a political game that dictates that we fit into a well-worn hierarchical structure from trainee to equity partner. As notaries, this will not do; you must be highly visible among your colleagues, contacts and potential clients.

There's no benefit to being visible if you don't know what you want to say, why and to whom. That's just creating noise. To what extent do you exist as a notary? Do people know who you are and what you do? What do you think they know about you?

Marketing

Marketing as a notary is relatively easy but, as a rule, notaries don't market themselves well at all. One possible reason for this is that notaries assume they will naturally get all the work available, or at least a fair share of it. Another reason is that notaries misunderstand the Faculty Office rules regarding marketing and don't want to risk doing anything wrong. Some notaries don't want to stand on another notary's toes or raise their heads too high above the parapet. Perhaps you don't know what to say or think that very little changes in notarial practice and don't know how interesting this legal sphere will be to non-notaries. Or perhaps, like me, you find the whole business of social media (an essential marketing tool these days) to be a bit tiresome and arduous. For most notaries, the reason that they do not market effectively is that they overcomplicate it and then procrastinate.

Target market and audience

In developing your marketing strategy, you need to identify two overlapping but distinct groups of people: your target market and your audience.

As a notary, you do not need to be visible to all people. You do not need to be a celebrity. You need to be visible to the right people. The first stumbling block for most notaries is not knowing who their target market is. We fall back on the idea that we are a public service and, therefore, everyone is a potential client. They are not. Few people need to use a notary. Most people will go their whole lives without requiring these services. It is a mammoth task to try to be visible to everyone, and a much simpler project when you decide in advance who you want to be visible to.

The audience for your marketing is not necessarily the same as your client base or your target market. You do not need to be speaking directly to your potential clients. You need to be speaking to your 'marketing army', who will pass the message on to your ideal clients. For example, if you are targeting commercial clients, you don't necessarily need to be addressing them directly. All commercial clients will have an existing relationship with a commercial solicitor and are likely to turn to that trusted professional when the requirement for a notary arises. You need to be at the forefront of the minds of the commercial lawyers in your area if you are to build a highly successful commercial notarial practice.

In identifying your audience, there will be obvious targets. This is the low-hanging fruit that you have easy access to, but make sure that this is in keeping with your ideal practice blueprint. Solicitor-notaries, this will be the clients of your law firm and your marketing army here is primarily the other solicitors in your practice and the marketing department, if you have one.

When thinking about your marketing army, refer back to your ideal client base. How could you position your message to reach the right eyes and ears? Think also about your USP – for instance, if you speak another language, could you use this in your marketing?

Your location

Most people who find a notary will have googled the words 'notary public' and a city or town. Type this into Google and see if and where you appear. Google Ads can be effective if you want to be top of the page. Many people will call the first name and number that they see.

Local law firms can also be part of your marketing army. Other law firms in your area that do not have a notary will be pleased to be acquainted with you and I have found that often the right person to know is the receptionist. Most of my referrals from other law firms have not come from the solicitors directly but from the reception staff. You can make this even easier by providing them with a stack of notary business cards to hand out. If you are a solicitor-notary, it is perhaps more diplomatic to have separate business cards for your notarial practice and your solicitor practice. Once you have delivered these to the local law firms, diarise the task of replenishing them regularly. If you work in a large city, you can decide who your 'local' law firms are.

If you have a particular source of work in your locality, and this fits into your ideal practice blueprint, find out who the influencers are in that community. For example, when I ran a practice in Leeds, I dealt with a large number of documents for India. Overseas Citizen of India visas had just been introduced and I made it my business to know everything there was to know about the supporting affidavits required. I also set a marketing mission to meet and become known to the most influential leaders in the local Indian community. This was not at all difficult as I was providing a highly valuable service. The easiest way to find out who these influencers are is to ask your clients. I did the same thing with the swathes of doctors applying to register in Australia. They all knew each other.

I handed out four business cards to every client and they were happy to recommend me.

Professional reputation

Once you know who you want to be visible to, you've identified your target market and your audience and have their attention, you need to decide how you want to be perceived. Your professional reputation is the story you are telling about who you are and what you do. It is also what people say about you, how they introduce you to people and how they regard you. It affects every aspect of your practice, from the clients you attract to the fees you can charge, your authority and your influence. It is everything.

Getting a reputation is not a passive project. You can choose your reputation but then you must actively build it. You have to decide how you are going to position yourself. Even if you have a well-established notarial practice, you can directly influence your reputation by adjusting your marketing and branding. At any stage in your career as a notary, you can devise, develop and maintain your professional reputation.

Thinking specifically about your ideal notarial practice that you have designed, what reputation would you need to have to create that practice with ease? For example, if you want to work with top-tier law firms and commercial clients in your area, charging substantial fees and being the first-choice notary, what reputation would you need to have? If you want to work from home and be the go-to notary for all private client work, what qualities would you need to display? If two solicitors were talking about you, what would you love for them to say? What would be the worst thing that someone could say about you as a notary? Perhaps the opposite of this is the reputation that you want to build. We are creating superlative notarial practices and to do that, we need to be definite about what we want.

First impressions

Once you have decided what it will be, you must actively create the reputation that you want. Your reputation as a notary is comprised of every piece of information that anyone has about you. Some of this information is communicated subconsciously by your environment, the way you present yourself, the clothes you wear, your punctuality and precision. Other information is given verbally or directly.

It starts with how you introduce yourself. Many notaries do not have an accurate and useful definition of what a notary is. Typically, when asked what a notary does, the notary will say something that sounds clever but means nothing. It usually stops the conversation dead. To answer the question 'What is a notary?' you need to be able to explain it in a way that an eight-year-old would understand. You can expand and elaborate depending on your actual audience, but in its simplest terms, a notary is a lawyer who deals with legal documents that are going to be used abroad.

When you explain what a notary is, you need to do it in a way that benefits you. Depending on your audience, you can state, 'I am an internationally recognised lawyer,' or you might say, 'I stamp documents,' or 'I am a lawyer and I advise on international matters.' Imagine that this person is going to introduce you to someone else. They are going to struggle with, 'This is Katherine, she authenticates documents for use overseas.'

If you give an example of the type of work you do, this should help build your reputation. If your ideal practice is mainly commercial clients, make sure that you provide an example that leads you this way. Don't talk about powers of attorney for Spain; say that you assist companies with their international legal transactions.

Presentation

How you present yourself also contributes to building your reputation. If your office is messy, your documents are scruffy or your marketing is non-existent, this is all feeding into the impression that you are making. Your website, your social media profile picture, even the pen that you give clients to sign documents with – these are all things that influence your reputation. You have to see yourself in the way that you want other people to see you. As a first-class notary running a highly profitable practice, you have to set your standards high and conduct yourself accordingly.

If, like me, you are reluctant to be on camera and rarely take 'selfies', you might need a bit of a reframe when it comes to being visible. Are you OK with people knowing what you look like? This is the fastest way for your clients, potential clients and your marketing army to make a connection with you. We like what we are familiar with and your audience will want to know what you look like. Not to judge you, but to make sense of what you are saying. Imagine going to see a speaker on stage and you are stuck behind a pillar. You can still hear them perfectly but you cannot see them. It's just not as powerful. You do not need to be 'perfect' to be visible.

Let people know what you look like, what you sound like, what you think and how you can help them. Perhaps book a photographer to take some great photos that you are happy to put on your website and social media. This is an excellent investment.

CASE STUDY: Jeremy

Jeremy is a full-time notary based in London. He is not a scrivener but he speaks four languages. He is bright, hard-working and ambitious, and wants to be one of the top notaries in London. Due to his location, Jeremy will have to work particularly hard to be seen and heard. He needs to use social media, traditional marketing and in-person networking to become known as a key person in the profession. He must become comfortable with having his photo taken and devise a bold marketing campaign that he applies consistently. He should use his language skills within his marketing and publish interesting relevant content every week. This will be a huge time and energy commitment but it will elevate Jeremy's reputation to the upper echelons of the profession.

Your message

Once you have chosen your audience and determined the reputation that you want to create, you need to decide your message. What do you want to say and why? Does this align with your practice blueprint? Will this get you the result you are looking for? What you say and how you say it determines whether or not you will build the reputation that you believe would create the business that you want.

It starts with understanding how people see you now – if they see you at all. If you have chosen to be visible on social media, for example, are you opting to be authoritative on interesting, relevant topics that will further your business? Or are you wasting the opportunity by engaging in small talk? You have to decide on your core message, which should be moving you towards your ideal practice not further away from it. Everything must be on brand.

As a first-class notary public who is building a formidable reputation as an expert, internationally recognised lawyer, you have plenty to say. Don't waste your opportunities. Your knowledge is your superpower – be generous with it. As you are creating visibility here more generally and not trying to gain clients directly, you don't need to be selling your services. That takes some of the pressure off. It is easy to make the mistake of being overtly 'salesy' in your marketing. You have already identified your audience and decided how you want to come across; your message is the medium through which you'll achieve your objective.

CASE STUDY: Victoria

Victoria is a private client solicitor-notary in a medium-sized city with two or three other notaries. She is at a stage in her career where she would like to be seen as a significant player in the local legal sphere. She wants to be recognised in the local business community and known as being 'brilliant, sharp and connected'. She is aiming to build a large client following and manage a fantastic, efficient and profitable team. Her message needs to be that she is knowledgeable, succinct and relevant. As she is not selling her services, she can use her marketing opportunities to demonstrate these qualities. For example, she could announce new legislation and give her intelligent opinion on it. She cannot build a reputation as someone sharp and brilliant if she is not willing to be judged. She can demonstrate that she is well connected by engaging with other sharp and brilliant people.

In the case study above, you can see how it would be off-brand for Victoria to be posting on social media about her cat waking her up too early. You must be willing to be visible but for all the right reasons. You've got to step up to being an expert and an authority. You will need to have an opinion on things related to your area of law so that you are regarded as in-the-know and 'the' person to ask. The quickest way to create this reputation is to be this person. Don't try to create this impression superficially. You must be bold and put yourself out there.

To craft your message, you don't need to change your personality or become incredibly sombre and serious. It is nice to show some frivolity, but this should not be the foundation of your reputation. Think of someone that you know, respect and admire. What is this person's message? Can you see how they have used it to build their professional reputation?

CASE STUDY: Aidan

Aidan is a solicitor-notary in a regional town. He has gotten rather bogged down in the day-to-day grind and has forgotten his potential and aspirations. He is a lovely man, friendly and knowledgeable. However, if he is truly honest with himself, he has let his standards slip a little in terms of his interactions with people and has become quite negative. If he imagined his peers discussing him, he would love them to use words like 'dynamic' and 'intelligent', but suspects he is not actively demonstrating these qualities at present. They are still a part of who he is and, when he is being dynamic and intelligent, he is in his element. By just bringing these aspects of himself to the fore, he can reignite his passion and alter his trajectory with a personalised marketing strategy. Then, this will be how he is regarded because this is who he is. His message needs to be: 'I have interesting, thought-provoking opinions on subjects that matter. I am intelligent and up to date on current legal affairs. My legal practice is efficient and correct.'

Summary

It is essential to be visible as a notary because few people know about us. We are a small legal profession and we have to shout nice and loud, at the right times, in the right place and to the right people. This requires a robust marketing strategy, with a clearly defined audience, a strong marketing army and an excellent professional reputation.

In creating your reputation, consistency is key. If you want to be known as professional but approachable, this theme must be prominent in all that you do. It must be evident in how you dress, how you hold yourself, how you speak and what you say. You must think about what you want to say and what impact you want to have so that your message is clear. To be visible as a first-class notary, you must decide how you want to be seen, who you want to be seen by and what you want them to see.

ACTIONS

Ask yourself:

1. How visible are you currently as a notary? How easy is it to find you online?

2. Are you open to being more visible as a notary? What would this take?

3. Who is your target market? Where is your marketing army? And who is the audience for your marketing?

4. How would you like to be regarded as a notary? Does this align with your practice blueprint?

5. What does your core message need to be to create your ideal reputation as a notary?

FIVE
Be Expert

As a notary, you are automatically an expert, even if it does not always feel that way. If you are in the first few months of your practice, you may feel that you are still grasping for competence rather than expertise. As an experienced notary, you may have niggling doubts about your procedures and practices, but believe me when I tell you: you are an expert.

Even so, there is more work to be done. As we progress in our notarial careers, we can start to feel somewhat jaded and our thirst for new knowledge and skills can be lacking. However, a first-class notary public requires an excellent attitude to change and learning and you must commit to being at the cutting edge of the profession. You cannot run a first-class practice otherwise.

When you can see yourself as an expert and raise your standards to reflect this title, your whole practice will rise accordingly. Your influence and reputation will expand, more opportunities will present themselves, your confidence will increase and your business will skyrocket.

You don't need to worry about what anyone else thinks. If you are afraid that others will think you are arrogant or delusional, just put this to one side. We all have self-doubt and anxiety, but to run a first-class notarial practice, you need to push on regardless.

Recognise your expertise

Your qualification as a notary is your niche. You must be seen by others as a specialist and that starts with seeing yourself as one. To your solicitor colleagues and contacts, your notarial status is your specialism, or at least it should be. You need to treat it with appropriate deference. Too often I see notaries acting as though their notarial qualification was just an accidental addition. They are dismissive of their special knowledge and skills, and often this comes across in how they run their practice.

Being an expert starts with how you view and describe yourself. If you are not yet comfortable with calling yourself an expert, you need to at least state that you are a specialist. You *specialise* in dealing with legal documents that are going to be used abroad.

In addition to being a specialist in this particular area of law, you also need to be an expert among notaries. To build a first-class legal practice that will generate profit, time-freedom and career flexibility, you must carve yourself a specialism within a specialism. This will not cut you off from any area of work but it will elevate your position as a notary, which will increase your influence, marketing opportunities and confidence.

Find a specialism

To be an expert, you don't need to know more than everyone, just more than most people about a specific subject. That might be overly simplistic, but it is true. As a notary, you need a specialism to elevate your position within the industry and establish your client niche. You do not need to be the only notary in the jurisdiction that has a special interest and insight into that topic. You just need to be in the class of notary experts on that particular subject and then let yourself be heard. It is no use having a secret specialism.

If you have a relevant specialism as a solicitor, this may be a good place to start. If not, you will need to pick a subject and set out to learn more about it than almost any other notary that you know. You do not need to be the number one authority on the topic, but you should be looking in that direction and put yourself on a par with the notaries that you consider to be the authorities. It does not need to be an academic legal subject; it could be a practical or technical matter, such as social media, governance or accounting. Devise a plan to increase your knowledge on your chosen subject and then demonstrate that you are an expert notary in this area.

Make it your business to be the 'go-to' person for something, but make it logical. For example, if you are a shipping lawyer, be the notary expert on shipping protests. If you are a private client lawyer, build an in-depth understanding of Court of Protection issues, or cross-jurisdictional probate or child abduction laws.

Imagine the Notaries Society Council discussing a difficult issue and wondering which notary they should refer to for advice – what would you like them to come to you for? If you have language skills, this is an excellent place to start. If you are qualified in another jurisdiction, this is your specialist skill. If you think that you are a general notary without any obvious areas of expertise, speak to other notaries and see what you might be missing regarding your USP.

CASE STUDY: Antonio

Antonio is fairly young and newly qualified. He does not know everything yet about notarial practice, but he speaks four languages fluently. Because he was not born in the UK, he does not fully appreciate how impressive this is. To most British people, this kind of language ability is a magical and elusive quality.

Being fluent in four languages is a superpower. It makes Antonio special, and this is his platform. Even people who do not need his language skills will regard him as belonging to a different class of notary if he is willing to showcase his expertise.

If you don't have anything on which you can hang your specialist hat, you will need to devise your specialism. This takes a little discipline, focus and effort. For example, you can be the expert on the e-apostille, or training, supervision, inspections or NotaryPro. If you cannot identify anything that would make you worth talking about, read the most boring and important legislation that you can find – the stuff that no one else can bring themselves to read – you will become invaluable. Anti-money laundering legislation is a great example. If relevant, think about how this approach could benefit your solicitor practice too.

Just make it your business to be an expert on something. It does not matter what it is as much as it matters that you have *something* that elevates you above others. My specialism is business development. I love to help other notaries to improve their practices. My superpower is weeding out the one thing that is holding the notary back and addressing this limiting belief or habit head on. I can also identify the notary's superpower that often they are failing to make use of.

When you have a specialism, you have a platform. As a first-class notary public, you have to be perceived as an expert among experts. It is illuminating how distasteful or uncomfortable this can feel. We are trained to be humble, which may be a prized characteristic at a dinner party but is of no use to you as you build your reputation, business and career. It is not arrogance. You have the credentials and knowledge to back up your claims. This is about recognising your attributes and allowing other people to benefit from them.

CASE STUDY: Rebecca

Rebecca thinks she is a standard notary. She does not have languages or any particular experience that puts her above any other notary. She works in a small, coastal town with no specific community. However, Rebecca wants a first-class notarial practice, and she wants to put herself on the map. Rebecca is young and has grown up with social media. She understands Instagram, Facebook and LinkedIn in the same way that other people know how to read the Financial Times or do cryptic crosswords. She instinctively knows how to take a selfie and how to build an online presence. She knows how to create a reel and upload an infographic. Not only can she do this for herself, but she can also run a masterclass for other notaries. This is a superpower. She can use her knowledge of social media to run powerful marketing campaigns and she can become well known among other notaries by showing them the basics of social media in a way that they can understand and appreciate.

Enforce high standards

In addition to having a notarial niche, you need to set a high standard for your practice. No expert sends out sloppy documents from their office. They do not attend meetings unprepared. If you are going to run a first-class notarial practice, you must commit to being a first-class notary.

When do you feel less than first class? For me, it is when I am rushing to get to the Post Office. There's nothing that makes me feel less adept and more out of control than standing in a queue with my Special Delivery envelopes, feeling harassed and running late.

The standard that you set for your practice filters down to everything that you do. It affects the clothes that you wear to see clients, the appearance of your office, your invoices, your communication, your emails and your telephone manner. Everything. It governs how quickly you respond to clients, your voicemail facility and your record keeping. A first-class notarial practice must have appropriately high standards in everything that it does. Nothing is exempt. The reason for this is that you are building your reputation, and your reputation dictates what opportunities are available to you. It determines the fees that you can charge and the clients you attract. Collectively, it is how we create our reputation as a profession.

You are creating your own version of a first-class notarial practice, designed to your own blueprint. It is up to you to define what a high standard means to you, though there are a few non-negotiables, which I'll discuss below.

Complex instructions

You must be willing to tackle the more difficult instructions. Expert notary publics do not shy away from anything. That's not to say that they don't want to. We all have thorny matters from time to time that make the cogs in our brains creak and whirl, and of course, we all prefer things to be straightforward. However, as an expert, you have to be able and prepared to step up when required. Expert notaries do not leave the taxing enquiries or troublesome matters to others. The advantage of being an expert is that you will have more referrals and greater opportunities to engage in the most lucrative instructions.

Precedents

Your precedents are the foundations of your practice. Do they work? Are they technically correct? Do they contain any extraneous information that detracts from the modern commercial nature of the document? Is this in any way helpful to the recipient of the document overseas?

Your precedent bank is not a one-time project. It is a functional machine that needs regular attention and fine tuning. Some notaries work from the premise that a notarial certificate needs a certain number of words to be legitimate and worthy of the fee, so they clutter up their document with unnecessary details that add little, if anything, to the notarial act. As an expert, you must be able to produce precise documents.

Regarding your blueprint for your ideal notarial practice, what precedents and systems would you need to have in place to make it a reality? Most things are easy to fix if you are willing to address them. Even reviewing or creating your precedent bank does not need to be a huge project.

Legalisation

Your legalisation systems must also be precise. When a client asks you, 'When will the documents reach Germany?' you should know the exact day. I appreciate that there are several moving parts to the legalisation process, but you have probably completed this process hundreds of times and the client has not. If you are sending the document by Royal Mail Special Delivery tomorrow morning, you can expect it to be with the legalisation agent the following day, legalised and ready for collection the day after and dispatched by courier later the same day. You already know the courier delivery estimation (or you can find out if you are willing to take the extra minute), which means that you can tell the client with confidence that you expect the document to be in Germany by Tuesday. This is all the client is asking you for. Give them the gift of certainty and let them lean on your experience.

Documents

You should be proud of the documents that leave your office. You must set an extremely high standard for yourself that you observe consistently, and train the staff that work with you to reach that same standard. You must start again with documents that do not reflect your level of expertise. While the appearance of the document is not the most important thing about it – the function of the document is far more important than the style and aesthetics – the standard you set for your documents is the standard you are setting for your whole practice. You cannot run an excellent practice and produce shoddy documents.

The equipment and materials that you use for your documents should reflect your high standards. For example, the paper that your documents are printed on needs to be sufficiently high quality. The stitching on your documents needs to be neat and functional. The purpose of the ribbon is to bind the document securely; it is not intended to be a free-flowing decoration. If it is not making the document more secure, why have you attached it? The ink stamps must be nice and black, not messy or faded. They must also state the correct information. A new ink stamp will cost you very little. If you don't have the right set of ink stamps, get them ordered today. Place your wafer in the right place, not haphazardly, and minimise the amount of writing that you are adding to the document. Imagine that each document is going to be intercepted and judged by another notary – would you be proud of the document that is leaving your office?

Your documents are one of the primary tools with which you are building your reputation and establishing your expertise. Make them exemplary, with no unnecessary flourishes.

The Faculty Office

To become an expert notary, understanding of and compliance with the Faculty Office rules and regulations is essential. You should also get to know the Faculty Office staff and understand who is governing us. Far from something to be intimidated by, our governing body offers a wealth of resources and guidance that can hugely elevate your expertise if you choose to take advantage of it.

Faculty Office rules and regulations

The rules and regulations that govern notaries in England and Wales are written by lawyers, for lawyers. We could not be more fortunate. They are incredibly easy to comprehend; it is not pages and pages of extraneous text. Once you have read them, other notaries will come to you for advice and you will be regarded as 'the notary that knows' – just because you took thirty minutes to download the Practice Rules and read them once a quarter.

In addition to the Notaries Practice Rules,[3] you should familiarise yourself with the Code of Practice[4] and other regulations that govern your notarial practice. Again, there is nothing difficult in any of them. Instead of living in quiet dread of a random inspection, read the Inspection Regulations and you will have the answers before you ever have to sit the exam. As an expert in notarial practice, you should be incredibly confident about the way that you are running your practice. If there is anything that you are not sure about, there are people you can ask. That's the beauty of our profession: it is exceptionally inclusive and helpful. I am sure that no one is going to faint with horror if you admit that you have a question.

Once you have read and understood the Faculty Office rules and regulations for yourself, you will be more confident in your practice. Many notaries work with a vague or niggling doubt that they are not quite sure what they are doing. I can understand this. Many of our systems were created and implemented when we

3   The Faculty Office, *Notaries Practice Rules* (2019), www.facultyoffice. org.uk/wp-content/uploads/2023/10/Notaries-Practice-Rules-2019. pdf, accessed November 2023

4   The Faculty Office, *Code of Practice*, www.facultyoffice.org.uk/ notaries/code-of-practice, accessed November 2023

first qualified and have been on rinse-and-repeat ever since. When you read the Practice Rules, you can adjust your ways of working if necessary or be reassured that you are doing things correctly. This is essential when you are running a first-class notarial practice. No one wants to draw attention to themselves unless they are confident that they know what they are doing.

Staying up to date

The Faculty Office frequently posts information on its website. This is one of the easiest ways for notaries to keep up to date. Diarise a task to click on the website once a week and you will be amazed at how quickly you will elevate yourself as a notary. Do the same thing with the Notaries Society website. You will be pleasantly surprised at how easy it is to become the notary who knows. When the Faculty Offices issue a consultation paper, it is because our governing body wants our opinions on something that they are thinking about doing or changing. Why wouldn't you want to be part of this conversation? As a first-class notary public, your opinion matters. Your contribution is important and valid. Let your voice be heard and valued.

CASE STUDY: Edward

Edward qualified as a notary a long time ago and, although he is highly regarded and accomplished as a solicitor, he has never been entirely confident regarding his notarial practice. He became a notary because his solicitor supervisor was one and it was a natural progression for him to do the same. He does not feel that his training was particularly thorough, but he is not sure where the gaps are or how he would fill them. He is due to retire as a solicitor in the next couple of years and would love to continue as a notary.

Within three months, with a little diligence and discipline, Edward can get up to speed with all the Faculty Office guidance. Once he has familiarised himself with the main rules and regulations, the Code of Conduct will give Edward all the information that he needs to feel confident in his procedures and reassure him that he knows everything necessary to run a first-class practice.

Your expertise is what will get you talked about in positive terms. When two notaries are chatting and your name comes up, what do you want them to say? What do you want to be known for?

Summary

To run a first-class notarial practice, you must be an expert. The first person who must recognise this quality is you. You need to be comfortable with this title to wear it well. As a notary, you are already an expert; when you have a specialism, you are both an expert *as* a notary and an *expert notary*.

You cannot simply call yourself an expert. You must make it your business to continually learn and gain experience and knowledge in a specific field that inter-ests you and is beneficial to your business. You must find a niche within your niche. Once you have picked your specialist subject, you must demonstrate your knowledge by sharing your information and insights at every opportunity.

As an expert, you must also uphold high standards in everything that you do, in your precedents, systems and documents. You should never shy away from complex instructions and should stay up to date and compliant with all Faculty Office rules and regula-tions, making use of their resources and guidance to stay on top of your game.

ACTIONS

Consider the following:

1. What is your existing or potential area of expertise as a notary?

2. How do you describe your role as a notary?

3. Is your notarial practice currently exhibiting excellent standards? What could you do to improve?

4. Do you have easy access to the Faculty Office rules and regulations? Have you read and understood them?

5. What platforms can you use to demonstrate your expertise?

SIX

Be Efficient

Almost all inefficient systems that are running in notarial practices are bad habits that have built up over time. An inefficient practice is a drain on your precious resources of time, mental clarity and money. An efficient practice has the right systems in place to maximise time and profit while providing an excellent service to clients.

A notarial practice can only be highly profitable if it is run like a well-oiled machine. Efficiency is doing the right thing, at the right time and in the right way. For a notarial practice, this means that you must be systematic in the way that you manage clients and enquiries, how you produce documents and how you process invoices and create records. It does not take much to throw it off and with relatively small profit margins, we must be disciplined in ensuring that everything we do is efficient.

As notaries, we can spend an inordinate amount of time repeating ourselves. This rinse-and-repeat action can give you a false sense of security because you can operate on autopilot, but if you are repeating the wrong things or unnecessary things, it is easy for your trajectory to quickly become inefficient. As you get busier, all the little inefficiencies add up and this is what can make notary work tiresome and unprofitable.

In my practice, I think about every element of what we do and we are constantly striving for new and better ways of doing things. This can be annoying to staff but every day we make a new distinction. We are permanently on the lookout for things that disrupt the flow of our notarial engine and seeking out ways to streamline. Every template email that we use is scrutinised to see where we are introducing ambiguity or duplication. Every problem or mis-understanding that presents itself – and there are many – is analysed to see why it occurred and how it can be fixed.

We do the same things in the same way, over and over. This might sound boring but it is the antidote to the tedium of having to repeat information or deal with slow instructions. We process a large number of docu-ments in our practice so we have to be meticulous in ironing out inefficiencies. Even so, I am sure we have only just scratched the surface.

What does efficiency look like to you?

In your practice, you will have your own pain points. In creating an efficient practice, you are working towards your ideal business so this is a highly personal project. You don't need to do things the same way as another notary; you need to make your practice work for you. As a first-class notary, you are aiming to have time-freedom, which means that you decide how, when and where you work. Time-freedom can only be achieved when your notarial practice is running smoothly. I find that many time-consuming tasks within a notarial practice have been accepted as 'the way things are'. If we have never seen a well-run notarial practice, we might not know just how smoothly they can operate. As solo operators, we could easily go our whole careers without seeing how other notarial practices are run.

Most notaries assume that they are already doing things pretty well. They allow around thirty minutes for each appointment and may have a payment system that is working OK. Sometimes their appointments run over, and now and then they may convert a notary client to a client of their law firm and, more often than not, clients turn up with the right documents. Most notaries have accepted that notary work is disruptive to their solicitor work, that enquirers need to speak to them personally and that clients may be late to their appointment and produce various curveballs within the meeting, such as an expired passport or a couple of extra documents.

Small changes, big impact

Often, inefficiencies just seem like little niggles and irks that do not warrant a 'solution'. Perhaps we have to change a precedent slightly every time we use it, or the ink stamp always leaves a little bit of the wording off, or the photocopier is often out of paper. Just a few seconds here and there. Give yourself the gift of the correct stationery, equipment and technology.

A first-class notarial practice does not tolerate the energy drain that is ineffective technology. Make a list of everything that you use and rate it as inadequate, sufficient or brilliant. Then you can formulate a plan to upgrade anything that is falling short. A belligerent printer can ruin an otherwise great practice. If you need to duplicate your stationery because you work from more than one location, do so. Keep a good stock of everything. Notaries only need a few items, there's no excuse for allowing yourself to run out of anything.

As you address all the things that cause drag in your notarial practice, you will see that it does not take much to pull your practice into a profit deficit. A first-class notarial practice must maximise its profit. The more inefficiencies you identify and fix, the slicker your practice will become. It soon becomes addictive. You will not tolerate anything being out of place. You will see potential improvements everywhere, and the way you do anything is the way that you do every-thing. You will see the same inefficiencies and errors in your solicitor practice. You will notice in other areas of your life ways in which you are not doing the right things, in the right way at the right time.

Staying, though, with your notarial practice, let's look at some of the areas you can focus on in your efficiency drive.

Enquiries

A good place to start is the initial client enquiry. This will typically be received by email or phone call, and the enquirer will either be an existing client or a new contact. The purpose of a phone call should be to estab-lish who the person is and create an email enquiry so that all your new matters are coming to you in the same way and can be dealt with systematically.

It does not need to be the notary that deals with the initial enquiry. There are so many ways to make this aspect of your practice more efficient and, there-fore, more profitable. You can train an assistant to follow a specific script. In the beginning, they will be pulled off script frequently – the clients won't be easily wrangled – but with continued discipline and consistency, they will get into the groove of quickly capturing the client's details, requesting the document and instruction by email and opening a file. If you can train someone to follow a script and show them exactly how to respond to the questions of how much and how quickly, all your phone enquiries can be converted into email enquiries, which can then be reviewed and delegated.

In my practice, when we take phone calls, we say the same thing every time: 'Good morning, The Notary Solution, [name] speaking, how may I help you?' They will often say something along the lines of, 'I need a document to be notarised,' or 'Do you deal with apostille?' Our response is the same every time: 'Certainly. What is your name, please? And your email address?' The tone in which all of this is said matters. It is authoritative and certain and lets the caller know what is required of them.

Once we have the client's name and email address saved into our CRM system, which is open while we take the call on a headset, we email the client using a template requesting the document and the instructions. We explain to the client what we are doing and that they should forward to us the instructions email that they have been sent by their lawyer. We will then reply with a fee quote and offer them an appointment. We do not give fee quotes or explain procedures over the phone. We keep the phone calls short and functional to review the document ourselves, which is always more efficient than having the client try to explain the requirements.

As a solicitor-notary, I did not do any of this. I got constant messages asking me to call a client about a document that needed to be notarised. As a sole practitioner notary, I did not run my practice like this either. I was always scrambling to answer my phone in my bag, shushing a child with frantic gestures and having to listen to long-winded voicemails or trying to make appointments while on the move. This is a highly inefficient way to wade through new enquiries. The thing about notarial practice is that you must be fast in responding to clients to get the instructions. Either you lose the instruction or the client calls you again. More interruption and time wasted.

Bring an efficiency mindset to your appointments too. Take charge of the appointment and the documents – this is your gift to your clients. You are in a position of authority and it is your responsibility that the appointment runs on time and the documents are notarised correctly. It is in everyone's best interests for you to be strict, even bossy if necessary. I often say to clients who need to be managed, 'Let me be bossy for a few minutes and we will get everything done correctly.'

Profit

As a solicitor-notary, you may have accepted that your notary work is not as profitable as your solicitor work. This is a mistake. It may be true, but you do not need to accept it as necessarily so. If your notary work is not as profitable as your solicitor work, it means you are less efficient as a notary than you are as a solicitor. There are several possible reasons for this. A common one is that you are not seriously monitoring client conversion and retention and are not accounting for this in your profit metrics. Or you may have bought into the idea that the job is a public service and there is inevitably time wasted advising potential clients that do not actually need a notary. There is indeed non-chargeable time involved in being a notary, but this does not necessarily need to be *your* time, and there are ways to reduce it.

Templates

Template emails explaining why clients don't need a notary have been a great time saver for me. I would often spend a good ten minutes on the phone with a client trying to persuade them to use a solicitor rather than a notary, or, for example, to create a travel consent but not to get it notarised. This was helpful to the client but not to my practice, and nor was it the most efficient way to get the information across.

In my practice, we use template emails saved as signatures. We have about twenty templates but most practices would work efficiently with around eight to ten. When we get a new enquiry, we can reply immediately, choose the signature and press send. We use these for requesting documents and signing instructions, giving standard fee quotes, confirming appointments and dealing with many of our most frequent enquiries.

Two particularly useful email templates are called 'solicitor or notary' and 'travel consent'. We use these to explain when a solicitor can be used instead of a notary and when a notarised travel consent is required. We have worded the emails carefully so that they do not sound like auto-responders.

Delegation

Another reason why you may not be as profitable as you could be is that you are not part of a team and think you have to do all the work yourself. Consider the support system that is required to make your solicitor work successful; this is also true for notary work, which will be less efficient if you are trying to do it all yourself. You need to create and train a team, regardless of whether you are a solicitor-notary or a sole practitioner.

Rates

A further reason for the lack of profit could be that you are not charging appropriate rates. Perhaps you are more concerned with what other notaries are charging than with positioning your service above the competition. Your rates must be well thought out and appropriate for the service that you are providing. You can charge on a time basis or a fixed-fee basis, but the fee should be commensurate with the work undertaken and what you are facilitating. In theory, the more experienced you are, the less time it should take you; take this into account when you set your rates.

Once you have determined your fees, do not allow clients to haggle. It takes up far too much energy. You must be fair to all clients by charging the same rates for the same work. It is appropriate for your fees to increase over time. Don't be afraid to charge the correct commercial fee for your work.

CASE STUDY: Carrie

Carrie is a solicitor-notary with a notional hourly rate of £350 an hour. She is willing and able to spend four hours a week on her notary practice. If she answered all the emails and phone calls herself, this could easily use up two of the hours, leaving her one hour to see clients and one hour to deal with document preparation, legalisation and record keeping. This means that she would need to see four clients within her one remaining hour and charge each one £350 to see a profit. This does not add up. Taking into account her overheads, to be profitable as a notary she needs to bring in £1050 a week (charging for three of her four hours), and so needs to see four to six clients a week. For the sake of simplicity, let's say she needs to see six clients a week paying £175 each. This needs to be six twenty-minute appointments, the administration of which needs to be delegated. In designing the mechanics of her notarial practice, she must use the administrative team available to her and must take on the task of training them herself.

Time management

First-class notaries are experts at managing their time. My favourite time management tools to use in running my notarial practice are **time blocking, automation**, **batching** and **checklists**. If you can get into the habit of following a precise and reliable system that you can use like a flow chart, you can catapult your practice into a profit-abundant business that is a pleasure to run.

It is hard to be perky and creative when you are explaining what an apostille is for the six-millionth time, especially when the client thinks that they are introducing you to a new concept. However, seeing your notary practice thriving is invigorating and introducing new clients to your solicitor practice is hugely rewarding. Once you have mastered the mechanics of your notarial practice, it can be a lot of fun to play around with the marketing, client conversion and profit generation. That's why it is so important to make use of all the best time management tools available, even if it does not feel strictly necessary yet, because this is what will give you time-freedom and enable your practice to grow and evolve.

Time blocking

Time blocking is where you allocate time in advance for specific tasks. This is particularly effective for client appointments. When you stop asking clients when they want to come in and instead tell them, 'I have 11.20 on Tuesday or 13.40 on Thursday,' you will find that the client will choose one of those options. They may need to rearrange the rest of their day but you will not. In addition to client appointments, you can block out time for marketing, accounting, record keeping, document preparation, taking enquiries and dealing with emails. You may already do this with your solicitor work, but leave your notarial work to run riot. If you have an assistant, you can schedule time to deal with their queries all at once rather than getting emails and interruptions throughout the day. Solicitor-notaries will need to be disciplined in scheduling the tasks related to their notarial practice.

Automation

Unnecessary repetition is tiresome and draining, so one of the most important aspects of time management is eliminating duplication. Notary enquiries fall into a small number of categories, such as powers of attorney, commercial documents, closing documents, Companies House documents and pension documents. We can spend an inordinate amount of time repeating ourselves, but repeated tasks and communications can often be automated.

Automation is where you set up a solution to automatically deal with a common task. For example, your voicemail should have a message that will move the enquiry forward. You don't need to ask the caller to leave their name and number and a short message. This is just tradition. Instead, you could say something like, 'Thank you for calling [name of business]. We are available today to assist you. The fastest way to get a quote, information or an appointment is to go to our website and submit an enquiry. The notary will deal with these enquiries first. If you cannot submit an enquiry through the website, please leave your number and a member of staff can assist you.'

You can use email auto-responders that do the same thing, with a link to the enquiry section of your website. Ultimately, you want all enquiries to be in the same format so that you can work through them most efficiently.

Batching

Batching means that you do all of one type of task together so that you are not constantly switching between projects. For example, you might pay all your invoices on just two days of the month. You might send documents for legalisation only twice a week. You could do all your call backs at the same time, or all your document preparation for the next day. How you batch tasks and when you do them is down to personal preference and depends on what works for your practice. I have tried many different things over the years and it is just a case of figuring out what is most efficient for you.

Social media posts and writing articles are excellent tasks to batch because they allow you to get into the creative flow of writing. It can be hard, if not impossible, to stop your day-to-day operations to write a short article within fifteen minutes. However, be careful not to stockpile a job you don't enjoy so that it becomes a mammoth task. Batching itself must be done efficiently, taking into account how much of one type of activity you can tolerate and get done.

Checklists

Checklists are an invaluable tool for notaries. No matter how experienced you are, a physical checklist cuts out all the reliance on memory. It takes very little effort to create a series of checklists and the extra few seconds it takes to run through one can save a great deal of time further down the line if it prevents a document from being rejected because a passport has not been signed, a date has been missed or a signature omitted. We are all human and these little oversights are understandable but avoidable. If you deal with a lot of documents, checklists can also be used by an assistant to review documents before they leave your office.

Protecting your energy

Being efficient is not just about managing your time, but also your energy. Notarial work is high energy. The documents we deal with are almost always urgent or time sensitive and clients tend to be stressed, worried or excited. It is crucial that you retain your mental clarity and don't take on other people's stress as your own. I am empathetic by nature so I find it difficult not to shift all my boundaries to facilitate a client's requirements. I had a phone call not long ago from a client needing documents to be notarised for his wedding in Cyprus – he was leaving the next day. I was horrified and desperately trying to work out how we could rescue the situation. However, the client was calm and just said, 'We will have the ceremony out there and just get married in the UK if we have to.' Be careful to manage your stress levels and maintain healthy boundaries.

Your peace of mind is a valuable resource and it must be protected for you to run a first-class practice as a notary and as a solicitor, maintain your health and nurture your most important relationships with your family and friends. Part of running a successful practice is being able to manage when things go wrong. Most of the time, notaries are running independent practices – this is a big responsibility. Life does not always run to plan; children get sick, families have emergencies and we cannot fulfil our obligations to our clients. However, an efficient practice can cope with the unexpected because we have anticipated the disruption in advance. If everything is where it is supposed to be, we can easily pass the work to another notary or rearrange an appointment. When matters are properly documented, we do not need to keep everything in our heads.

Summary

Efficiency is a mindset. As you examine your notarial practice as it is currently, you will see obvious areas for immediate improvement that will benefit your bottom line. You need to eliminate anything that is not vital, delegate the tasks that someone else can do as well or better than you, automate everything that you can and batch similar tasks to be dealt with in bulk. Use checklists for every transaction and you will soon iron out those post-completion hiccups that take up so much resource. Remember that your energy is a resource that must be efficiently managed just as you manage your time.

When you're running an efficient practice, it is reassuring to know that a routine inspection would not be a problem. A first-class notary can be positively smug about an impending inspection and welcome the opportunity to demonstrate the smooth running of their compliant and thriving practice. You can be wonderfully self-assured when you are running an efficient notarial practice, and this enables you to focus your energy on the growth of your business.

ACTIONS

Consider the following:

1. What does an efficient notarial practice look like to you?
2. Are you handling initial enquiries in the most efficient way possible? Do you receive all enquiries in email form?
3. What tasks are you currently delegating? Is there scope to delegate more?
4. Can you automate any routine/repeated tasks? What tasks can you batch?
5. Are you/your team using checklists to ensure nothing is ever missed?

SEVEN
Be Bold

O nce you have an expert practice that is visible and efficient and you have positioned yourself as an expert, you must be bold in making your ideal notarial practice a reality. Being bold means so much more than being confident. It means embracing your fears head on and saying yes to the opportunities that present themselves to you as a result of your actions. It means leaving your comfort zone and stepping up to your full potential. It means accepting that the ideal practice that you have designed is within your capability.

You must be bold enough to approach the dream commercial clients; to say yes to the speaking opportunities; to engage with the committees that will elevate your status and influence; and to do whatever is required to enable you to enjoy a first-class notarial practice on your own terms. You must be able to say no to the people that you cannot serve; establish and enforce strong boundaries; charge appropriately and manage your workload in a healthy and scalable way. Solicitor-notaries must be brilliant at artfully introducing new clients to their law firm to increase their influence and create career flexibility.

You may ruffle feathers as you do this, and that's OK. It is not your aim but it is an inevitable consequence of disrupting the status quo. No matter who you are, fear may arise along the way. This is your brain's way of protecting you from danger. You may worry that you will get fired, get into masses of debt, or give up a promising and safe career as a solicitor to create your ideal notarial practice. Having done all these things, I can confirm that they are possibilities. However, you must bet on yourself to build a first-class notarial practice that generates ample profit, time-freedom and career flexibility.

Overcoming fear

The number one thing that holds notaries back is fear. Fear of the unknown, mostly. There are no guarantees with notary work. It is hard to know where the work will come from, and yet it does come. The antidote to fear is safety nets in the form of repeat clients, good contacts and other sources of income, but ultimately, if you want to swim, you have to lift your feet off the ground.

Is your blueprint for your ideal notarial practice sufficiently exciting and motivating? Is it a project that is worth starting and maintaining? If not, you need to revise it and include the missing elements that would make it so. If you can honestly say that this is something that you truly want and are willing to work for, then it is time to be bold in the execution of your plan.

Two words kill most ambitions and they are 'not yet'. Many of the notaries I have worked with over the years have brilliant plans but there is a gulf between where they are and the start of their plan. This is because there is no urgency. Their business plan remains theoretical. It's not a lack of time or knowledge. It is not a lack of resources. It is just a general feeling that the timing is not right. It never is. I am not encouraging recklessness but your plans and projects will come to nothing if you do not start. You must be able to push through discomfort and take your ideas from good intentions to completed actions.

In being bold, you need to recognise your fear and reluctance and press on regardless. The way I do this is I commit myself before I am ready. I announce the training course before I have written it. I pick up the phone before I know what I am going to say. This sometimes causes me anguish but it gets things done.

CASE STUDY: Helen

Helen is a competent notary who also works as a
solicitor. At the moment, she is not happy in either role.
The income from her notary practice does not reflect
the amount of work involved and she is often playing
catch up with her solicitor work because she has to
deal with the notary enquiries throughout the day.
She feels that the only way to excel as a solicitor is to
give up the notary work, which she is reluctant to do
given the amount of work that went into obtaining the
qualification. To align the two practices to effectively
complement each other, Helen will need to involve
the senior management team and explain to them the
benefits of having a notary at the firm. This makes
her nervous. She will need to redesign her notary
practice so that she can work with a team and actively
introduce new clients to the law firm. This is not her
usual style and it will take her outside of her comfort
zone. However, she knows that if she delegates
the administration and the queries and focuses on
improving her skills as a lawyer, she will ultimately be
where she wants to be in her career.

If you want a first-class notarial practice, you can have
one. You have all the tools and resources you need.
You must be bold to reap the rewards. There are various areas and ways in which you need to do this, to
prove your value – to yourself and others – we'll look
at some of those now.

Solicitor-notaries

Not all notaries want to be sole practitioners. Most solicitor-notaries love their work as a solicitor and want to turbo-charge that aspect of their career, but they may need to reframe their notarial practice as an asset to their law firm. This has to go beyond lip service. Solicitor-notaries, especially those who work in busy commercial firms, need to recognise the amazing cross-referral opportunities that their notarial work creates. Provided that you do an excellent job as a notary, you are in the perfect position to skilfully introduce your notarial client to other services that your firm can provide. This takes conscious thought and planning, but once you get into the habit of identifying cross-referral opportunities, it can be a rewarding aspect of your notarial practice.

Be a rainmaker

The most valuable person in a law firm is 'the rainmaker'. This is the person who can bring in new clients and business to the firm. It is regarded as a magical quality that only a few lawyers have and those that do have it, generally make it look effortless. I said at the beginning of this book that your notarial faculty is your magic wand and for solicitor-notaries, you can use it to bring in new clients to your law firm.

This is a skill that you can learn at any point in your career. It starts with intention. Anyone not currently a client of your law firm is a potential client and your intention must be to assist this client in any way that you can. There is always a service that you can offer. First, you must know and be familiar with every service that your firm provides. You must be an expert on your firm – the directors and the associates, the departments and the specialisms. You are going to become a master salesperson and you must know everything there is to know about the services available.

When you are the rainmaker in your firm, you do not need to do any other form of networking. When you bring clients into the firm, you increase your influence, respect and personal power. This creates career flexibility. Being a rainmaker gives you a choice about who you work with, how you work, when you work and where you work. It has a compound effect, increasing the options available to you.

Spotting opportunities

Once you know what your firm can offer, you need to match it to the requirements of the person in front of you. You are not selling for the sake of selling. You need to listen for the right opportunity and you must have the right patter. You are not a desperado trying to meet your sales quota. You are a master matchmaker, creating the connection between what the potential client wants or needs and what you have available.

As a notary, when we have a new client in front of us, our primary responsibility is to do a good job – even an excellent job. The person needs to trust that we know what we are talking about in the first instance, and that this is what we are being paid for. However, within the conversation, there is room to discover whether there is anything else you can assist with. You should have in mind the portfolio of services that you can offer, which may just be adding the client to a specific mailing list. Your job as a rainmaker is not to close the sale but to open it.

If you have the resources available, an elegant way to do this is to have an associate on hand to do the follow-up. For example, if you are doing a power of attorney for Spain, you should remind the client that if they are buying property in Spain, they need a Spanish will. This is a perfect opportunity to confirm that they have a British will in place that they are happy with. How easy it is to say, 'You should speak to Amanda in our private client team. She's lovely and she's brilliant at that sort of thing. Shall I ask her to drop you a line?' That's it. That's your job with the client completed. No hard sell is required or desired. Once you are out of the meeting, you hand the referral to your associate for immediate follow-up.

Demonstrating your value

As a notary, you must be able to demonstrate with facts and figures that you are bringing clients into your

THE NOTARY SOLUTION

solicitor practice. This means you need to follow each referral – you'll get no credit for potential or vague referrals. If you are a solicitor-notary, you should know before you see every notary client whether the person is an existing client of your firm. If they are local, it may be that your firm did their conveyancing for them ten years ago. You should know this information before you enter the room.

This must be done with complete integrity, of course. Your job is not to sell clients services that they do not need but to simply connect them with the right people to assist them. A rainmaker is in the right place, at the right time, saying the right thing in the right way to the right people. With commercial clients, your role as a rainmaker is to establish and maintain a professional relationship. You do not need to sell; you need to open a clear line of communication and know the services that your firm offers. This is enough; the instructions will come in due course.

CASE STUDY: Sia

Sia is a solicitor-notary who wants to create a notarial department in her firm, train a new notary and then work as a team to generate leads for her solicitor practice while creating a self-sufficient department in terms of profit and fees. She wants to be known in her city as a highly respected commercial notary and to integrate this with her solicitor work. She would also like to be elected to the Notaries Society Council, but she is not sure yet what this would entail.

106

Sia needs to add the new notary idea to the agenda for the next solicitor management meeting and to contact the Notaries Society to find out more about being elected to the Council. Nothing will change until Sia is willing to be bold in taking the steps required to create her vision.

Supervision

As a first-class notary, your practice blueprint must incorporate an element of teaching. The quickest and most effective way to raise the standard of your own notarial practice is to take on a supervisory role for another notary. Our profession grows organically. New notaries qualify but it is the responsibility of the rest of the profession to teach them, assist them and give them the tools that they need to thrive.

Every new notary that qualifies must complete a period of supervision. This is a formal arrangement with a qualified notary who meets the supervisor criteria set by the Faculty Office. It is the responsibility of the newly qualified notary to find someone willing to supervise and, unfortunately, this is not always an easy process.

Perceived scarcity

Three things seem to dissuade an experienced notary from agreeing to supervise a new notary. The first is a scarcity mindset and related fear that the new notary is going to reduce the work available to the existing notary. This is simply not true. In my experience, a new notary qualifying is always a boost to the profession. New notaries are generally brilliantly trained and highly knowledgeable. There are certain things, though, that they can only learn in the field and so they need the rest of the profession to be open, welcoming and supportive.

The experienced notary will benefit equally from the supervision arrangement. When we teach, we articulate our knowledge. We see our own practice with a fresh perspective that enables us to recognise what is working and identify what is missing. The supervisory process and experience are mutually beneficial.

Time

The second thing that discourages supervision is the notion that supervising someone will be too time consuming, especially for the busy solicitor-notary. Provided you are clear with the supervisee about the expectation that they take on any administrative burden themselves, such as typing up reports and arranging the requisite meetings well in advance, there is no reason why this role should be unduly onerous. You can encourage the notary to join a supportive network to assist with day-to-day queries but in general, you will find that time spent supervising is an investment that improves your practice.

I had two excellent supervisors when I was a newly qualified notary – Chris Hilton in Newcastle and Robert Bond in London – and I will always be grateful to them for shaping my practice and giving me the support and encouragement that I needed at the time. In addition to my supervisors, I had a wonderful notary in Newcastle called James Bowyer, who allowed me to call him with all my most basic questions in those early months. It was twenty years ago but I will never forget his kindness, patience and generosity. As a first-class notary, it is your duty and your privilege to supervise new notaries and you will find that it is time well spent.

Knowledge

The third thing that gets in the way of supervision is a niggling doubt that one is not entirely competent enough to teach, or the assumption that someone else will do a better job. If you are being asked, you are the best person for the job. You will surprise yourself with how much you know and will improve your knowledge further by working as a team with the new notary.

If done correctly, the experienced notary will learn as much from supervising as the newly qualified notary. They get an insight into the law that is being taught at university so it is a useful refresher for the notary. I think that providing supervision should be compulsory and supervisors should be allocated by

the Faculty Office. I don't think that the new notaries should have the daunting task of trying to shop
around for someone willing to supervise, as I'm sure
this can be disheartening. I would also change the
rule that it needs to be someone within the same geographical area. With modern technology and remote
communication, this is no longer necessary. Indeed,
it is potentially detrimental to the new notary's progression to be supervised by someone who may
consider them a rival – though of course, all notaries
who have read this book will know that this is not an
accurate perception.

Review your practice blueprint and see what teaching
roles you can include to build your first-class practice.
If you are eligible to supervise, register your availability with the Faculty Office.

Embracing change

As a bold, first-class notary, enjoying all the benefits
that this brings, you must make yourself heard and
be at the cutting edge of the profession. This is true
regardless of what stage you are at in your notarial
career. This has nothing to do with seniority, it is all
about attitude.

If you are willing to embrace change, you can create
a practice with longevity and resilience. If you resist
change, you will create a practice that is decaying

and brittle. This cannot possibly serve you. It will be vulnerable to competition and create stressed and defensive notaries that cling to inefficient and archaic ways of working. These notaries waste an unnecessary amount of energy complaining about how things should be and looking at what other people are doing instead of claiming their own power and focusing on solutions.

As a profession, we have a misplaced notion that not much changes in notarial practice. We complete training each year and may struggle to find anything new to learn. We don't particularly want anything to change. We want to plod on while we can with our stamps and our seals while being aware that at any moment, the entire profession could become obsolete if solicitors are accepted abroad in place of notaries. Therefore, for notaries, change can be a threat. We like things to stay the same, but a first-class notary is fully prepared for and able to benefit from change.

For example, at some point over the next few years, electronic documents will become the norm. We and our clients will sign documents electronically. We will also notarise and apostille them electronically. It may be hard to imagine, but then so was electronic document storage at one stage. When I started my career as a notary, we had a physical paper register in which we recorded each transaction. It was rather a nice time. I enjoyed neatly writing up each appointment. Clients paid by cash or cheque, which were the only options.

I paid them into the bank by visiting the counter in the branch. Now we don't accept either form of payment; everything is electronic.

Change is inevitable and natural. It only upsets us when we fight against or feel fatigued by it. New regulations will be introduced by the Faculty Office, identity checks will be modernised and yes, it is even possible that the profession will become obsolete. That's OK – we will simply have to focus our brilliant minds on something else. If you know that whatever happens, you will manage just fine, you can adopt a growth mindset and continue to thrive.

CASE STUDY: Graham

Graham is around eight years qualified as a notary and has a nice steady practice as a solicitor-notary. He knows what he is doing in both roles and is relatively comfortable. He is not averse to change but he does not go looking for it either. However, he would like his notary practice to be more dynamic. He is curious about electronic documents and utilising technology to grow his practice beyond his current locality.

Maintaining a curious mindset, Graham begins to explore how his practice can expand and be ahead of the curve. He reads all the material he can find on electronic signatures and educates himself on the terminology involved. He reviews the reports and guidance issued by the Faculty Office, the Notaries Society and the Foreign, Commonwealth and Development Office. He familiarises himself with other notaries doing the same thing and researches what notaries in other jurisdictions are doing.

Within a few months, Graham feels like he has become a bit of an expert in this area and, the more research he does, the more interested he is in what's possible. As an experiment, he starts to offer electronic services alongside his traditional practice and he quickly comes to be regarded as a frontrunner of change. He can apply the same open mindset to his solicitor practice and feels confident to implement his new knowledge by introducing electronic signatures, digital identity checks and electronic payment options.

A plan of action

The willingness to be bold is a mindset but also a practical exercise. It is action-orientated. In assessing your ideal notarial practice, you will identify several tasks that require you to actually do something. These are your 'action points', which together constitute your plan of action – your list of actions required to move your notarial practice from where it is to where you want it to be. For example, if you want to increase your fee income by 50% and double your profit margin, you will have a list of ideas on how to achieve this. This is not going to be ticked off your to-do list in one day, but you need a plan so you can make a start.

Ensure that the action points are 'actionable'. If you have a vague plan to 'make contacts' or 'do business development', refine it into something more tangible. An action item like, 'do a social media post' is unlikely to get done but 'write 500 words on (a pre-defined topic)' is unambiguous and non-negotiable. Some of these actions will be tedious and time consuming; some will feel uncomfortable and some will be beyond your control at this time. You do not know yet which of your ideas will create the result you want, so start with the most obvious upgrades and weave them into a plan of action.

Break tasks down into their smallest components, if this is beneficial to you. For example, if you need to hire a new member of staff, you are not going to do this in a morning. It is a process that needs to be broken down. If you have not been responsible for recruitment previously, you need to learn the steps involved to make it happen. Once you get into the habit of breaking down the high-impact goals into small actionable tasks, you build momentum.

At first, it all seems like a lot of hard work, and it is, but when you start to see the results, this justifies the effort required. An accountability partner is invaluable at this stage. Find an equivalent notary in another city and together work through the first six months of your plan. Most of the time, the resource needed is consistency. Sometimes, you just need to be brave enough to pick up the phone, write the email, order the marketing flyers, submit the article or put yourself forward for election. The more you do, the easier it gets.

Summary

Turning dreams into reality requires bold action. This can be scary, but you must overcome any fear so that you can start taking steps towards turning your blueprint into an actual practice. To do this, your motivation must be stronger than your fear – if it isn't, you may need to revisit your blueprint to ensure it is something worth taking risks and making yourself uncomfortable for.

For solicitor-notaries, you will need to be bold in identifying, creating and capitalising on opportunities for cross-referral within your law firm so that you can demonstrate and communicate your value. You should also be bold in putting yourself forward as a supervisor for new notaries entering the profession; this is a mutually beneficial relationship and allows you to stay up to date with your knowledge while establishing yourself as a leader in the profession.

A first-class notary is bold in facing the future, undaunted by impending change and ready to put their plans into action.

ACTIONS

Ask yourself:

1. What actions can you take in the next ninety days to move your notarial practice in the right direction?

2. Is there anything you haven't included in your practice blueprint that you would like to happen?

3. What is your main fear concerning your notarial practice? How could you counter this?

4. Are you willing to register your availability to supervise with the Faculty Office?

5. Do you have a practical strategy for offering your law firm's services to your notarial clients?

PART THREE
BUILD YOUR BUSINESS

Building a first-class notarial practice that generates abundant profit, time-freedom and career flexibility takes more than a great plan. Action is required to breathe life into your vision. You know what tasks need to be completed but you must make them a priority if your ideal notarial practice is to come to fruition. Your plan needs to be exciting enough to keep you motivated, and then you must be consistent in taking action towards it and willing to make adjustments along the way.

PART THREE
BUILD YOUR BUSINESS

EIGHT

Make It Happen

O nce you have designed your practice blueprint, you need to create it. This is where the hard work begins. It is so easy to extinguish all the momentum you have built up until now, simply by falling back into old habits or procrastinating and avoiding the actions required to make your plan a reality.

There will be times when you lack motivation – many times, in fact. Your solicitor work will take over; a family member may be unwell and need your attention; life will get in the way of your design. That's OK. This is inevitable and so needs to be factored into the overall plan. It's fine to go off course; this does not mean that you need to start again or abandon the plan entirely. You just need a way of bringing yourself back into line on a regular and consistent basis.

The starting point is to create a game plan that is exciting and fun. Not the words most often associated with notarial practice, I know. However, a first-class notarial practice has excitement and fun woven into it, whatever that takes. You also need to use persistence and patience and see your plan as a long-term project with interesting milestones. Finally, you need to appreciate that your plan is only your best guess right now at what will bring you abundance, time-freedom and career flexibility. You will need to review and adjust it along the way.

Get excited

By now you may be realising that the ideal practice plan you created at the beginning of this project was not ambitious enough. Everyone is unique and my version of an exciting game plan will be different to yours. No two notaries are the same but we assume that what we want, everyone else wants too. There may be some commonalities but, ultimately, we are inspired and motivated by different things. We want to work different hours, from different locations and with different people. We want to wear different clothes and decorate our offices to our tastes. What fires you up is individual to you.

Your vision

I love the idea of running a national notarial services company. I can picture the offices and the staff and how systematic and tidy it will be. The office is white with brightly coloured stationery. The head office is in Harrogate, within five minutes of my house. I picture it like a beautiful engine room. The staff are all smiling as they take calls on their headsets. There is a lovely coffee station with a biscuit barrel and I come and go from the office, which runs perfectly with or without me. I also have two other businesses that run in parallel with the law firm. We get five-star reviews daily and our happy clients enthusiastically recommend us to other clients. This is my utopian practice.

Yours will undoubtedly be different, but there must be a vision – something to make all of the work that you are going to do worthwhile. Perhaps you want to be in the top tier of solicitors in your area; to be known and to be influential. Maybe you have a vision of walking your kids to school each morning and picking them up each afternoon with a homemade snack ready for the walk home, starting work at 10.00 each day and finishing at 14.00. Perhaps you are a writer at heart and would prefer to spend your days writing novels and want your notarial practice to facilitate this. You might love the idea of surprising your spouse with an amazing trip to Italy, funded entirely by the additional income that your practice will create over the next year. Maybe you want a notarial practice department in your law firm that is considered to be an amazing resource for introducing new clients and generating consistent monthly fees.

Whatever it is that fires you up, use it. To build and manage a first-class notarial practice, you need an exciting practice plan, something that keeps you on course and pushes you to expand your comfort zone. Your plan will change over time. It does not need to be a definitive end point; you can revisit and refresh it whenever you need to.

Don't worry if envisioning your 'dream practice' feels self-serving; you will still help lots of clients, do a great job and be a good person. All we are doing here is creating a practice plan that *you* find exciting, to provide inspiration and get your creativity flowing. You don't have to share this with anyone if you don't want to; at this stage, it is just for you.

Be in it for the long haul

Your practice plan should be compelling enough that you don't mind whether it takes three months or three years. Provided you are moving towards it, it is a journey worth starting. You need to be able to see far into the future if you are going to have a first-class business that works for you on every level. This is your long-range lens. Your progress is unlikely to be linear and you will need to keep referring to your ultimate vision along the way.

A tool I love to use is the retrospective lens. I place myself in the reality that I want, really connect with it at a visceral level, and then look back to the present day. I can map the actions that I took and what I needed to do to get to that reality. This makes the route clear and shows me what I need to do this week, this month and this year.

Consistency

The key to thinking and acting for the long term is consistency. In notarial practice, this means always doing the right things, in the right way, at the right time. It is not enough to send out a marketing mailshot and then nothing else for eighteen months. You have to tend to your practice as you would a beloved garden – you don't expect to see flowers in spring if you don't plant them in autumn.

Consistency is my weakness. I tend to have bursts of huge enthusiasm that peter out like fireworks, as something else claims my time and attention. I know this, so I use tools that keep me consistent. I schedule meetings in advance. I publicly commit to actions that I am not ready for but know I want to take. I use apps, stationery, charts and the people around me to keep me focused on the tasks that need to be done to achieve my overall objective. If this sounds exhausting, that's because it is. Some people are naturally consistent, and it is not a huge effort for them. In fact, for some people, breaking their routine takes far more energy than keeping to it. Whatever it takes for you, you must be consistent in carrying out the actions necessary to create your first-class notarial practice.

CASE STUDY: Carlos

Carlos is a solicitor-notary who wants to move up a level in terms of income. He has a young family and aims to provide a certain lifestyle for them. He would love to take them over to see his family in Spain more frequently and to do so with a level of comfort and ease. This is the motivation that he needs to turbo-boost his notary practice and demonstrate its value to his solicitor colleagues in terms of client referrals and reviews. He decides that he wants to double his practice as a notary and although he does not yet know how he will do so, he believes it is possible.

Carlos recognises that his current way of working will not facilitate his plan so he signs up for new CRM software at a relatively small monthly fee. This enables him to dramatically increase the efficiency with which he is running his practice and to accept electronic payments. Because he has easy access to his figures, he can set targets and see a visual representation of his business income. He can be strategic, ethically introduce new clients to his law firm and highlight the existing clients who have been able to get documents notarised without going to another firm. Very quickly, he alters his career trajectory and is being considered for promotion within his firm.

Review and adjust

The plan that you have now may not work out exactly as you anticipate and that's OK. You are not clairvoyant and your plan is only your best guess, given the information and understanding you have available at the time. To create a first-class practice you need to review your practice plan on a regular and consistent basis, whether that's once a month or once a week. This requires that you sit down and consciously review your plan and your progress. Don't overcomplicate this. Don't rip up the plan and start again. All you need to do is get a cup of coffee, get out your plan and ask, 'Is it working?'

You will know immediately if you are happy with your plan and your progress. If you are not, you need to ask yourself what has gone off track. It will either be something you are doing that you shouldn't or something you are not doing that you should. Most of the time, it's that we haven't done the things we said we would do. The reason we give is usually that we are 'too busy', but what that really means is that we have prioritised other things.

For example, you may have within your plan a task to create a LinkedIn campaign and to post a weekly article about notarial practice, or your particular specialism within it, but after the first published post, this falls by the wayside. You will, I'm sure, have legitimate reasons for not following through on your plan, but be honest with yourself about these. You may have been disheartened by a lack of engagement with your post, or you simply haven't scheduled enough time and preparation to write and post the articles. You might have had a technical problem and haven't worked out the solution. For me, it is always that the task was not scheduled or I ignored the schedule because I wanted to do something else. I need someone to keep me accountable. I don't mind writing the article, I just find the act of uploading the post to be unduly arduous and stressful. I worry that I am going to get it wrong somehow or I agonise about the exact photo to use, as if it matters.

Diarise it

Like any project, building a practice is a constant and ever-evolving process, and it is important to know this from the start to avoid burnout and disillusionment. Like raising a child, in nurturing your notarial practice you will move from phase to phase and time will seem to evaporate. You look back fondly at each stage, conveniently forgetting the stress, anxiety and sleepless nights. Every year, your practice needs to be assessed and your plan updated. October is a great time to do this. As you are applying to renew your practising certificate, sit down with your team and reflect on the successes of the previous year, set your targets for the new practising year and adjust your practice plan.

You can share this with your accountability partner and create prescheduled checkpoints throughout the year. You have committed to creating a first-class notarial practice that works wonderfully for you and your clients. This requires your active involvement at the planning stage and needs regular review sessions to keep it on track.

Do *something*

When formulating a business plan, most people are wildly ambitious about what they think they will do, and notaries are no different. We may start off thinking that we will write one article a week, attend a networking event twice a month and engage with social media every day. That is a great plan, but if a reduced version of that means you can keep it consistent, treat that reduced version as a minimum and consider everything else a bonus. Therefore, start with your bare minimum plan. These are the most important tasks but in their minimum effective quantity. This is the version of your plan entitled, 'If I do nothing else, I will *definitely* do this.' It reduces your plan to critical actions.

This does take some of the fun out of it. Rebranding your stationery and website with a new logo and colour scheme has to wait patiently until you have scheduled your continuing professional education (CPE) and chased your outstanding accounts. Not all actionable items on your practice blueprint are equal.

As you review and adjust, you must be ruthless in prioritising the things that will have the most impact on the progression of your ideal notarial practice.

Summary

The energy required to create your first-class notarial practice is front loaded. You are going to have to put in a great deal of time and mental energy at the beginning, even if you have been running your notarial practice for some time. You have devised an exciting plan but it is going to require commitment from you to make it happen. You may not see the results of your hard work for a while and it will take time to build the reputation that you want, so you need to be in it for the long haul. Over time, things will change and you will need to review and adjust as you go. When you are reviewing your plan, all you need to ask yourself is: am I doing the things that I said I would do? Often it is too early to decide whether they are working yet.

Your first-class notarial practice is like a jigsaw; each action that you take creates another piece of the overall picture. No single action is sufficient to get the result you have visualised but you need to keep putting in the pieces anyway. Provided that you have your ideal practice mapped out in your mind, and you have checked your plan for incongruences with the rest of your life, each action just needs to be directionally correct and taken consistently.

ACTIONS

Ask yourself:

1. Do you have an exciting practice plan that you can't wait to get started on?

2. What are your most likely excuses for not following through? What can you do to counter them in advance?

3. What tools can you use to ensure that you are consistent in your actions?

4. If you do nothing else in the next ninety days, which three to six action points are you committed to completing?

5. Where do you see yourself one year from now, if you do the things that you say you are going to do?

NINE

Discipline

The biggest obstacle to realising your perfect practice is you. You have designed a wonderful notarial practice that is going to create abundant profit, time-freedom and career flexibility, provide an amazing service to clients and be a pleasure to run. It is going to positively influence every other area of your life and it is yours for the taking. Why would you not grab this with both hands?

The main reason is that life gets in the way. We treat this like a paper exercise that we will definitely get around to, and we genuinely believe ourselves. We fail to take the actions that will lead to the results that we want. We have legitimate reasons for this. We are all highly functioning and successful professionals; we would not deliberately sabotage our success, and yet we do. Consistently, reliably, repeatedly. Until we do something different.

Three tools that I have found the most effective in countering this tendency to self-sabotage and develop discipline are accountability systems, solid boundaries and staff training.

Accountability

If you are a solicitor-notary and you have a management meeting with your solicitor colleagues, there will be notes taken, action plans created and expectations set. Minutes will be circulated and you know that you don't want to be sitting at the next management meeting explaining why you haven't done the things that you said you would do. This is accountability. It creates a tension that isn't resolved until you complete the required action. It feels uncomfortable and that discomfort is a highly effective motivator. You can learn to love it.

People

As notaries, we are often 'solopreneurs'. That means there is no one to champion us when we do well and no one to chide us when we fail to follow through. However, we still need accountability, so we must create this community for ourselves. Start with a notary peer at the same level as you, someone with a growth mindset who wants to make positive changes in their practice. Ideally, choose someone outside of your locality so that you can talk freely without feeling defensive or protective. The whole point of this synergistic relationship is to create accountability and to motivate each other to take the actions that will have the biggest impact.

If you do not want to work with another notary, you can create an accountability partnership with another lawyer or businessperson. You can even pay someone to coach you. However, in my experience, working with another notary is most effective. Agree at the beginning of the relationship how you will end it. You can start by committing to, say, a three-month project, keeping each other accountable over that period, and then see at the end whether you want to embark on a second project together. It's similar to how you would work with a fitness coach.

Systems

Another way to create accountability that doesn't involve others is through systems. A business coach that I work with introduced me to the 'got it done list'. Every time he completed an action, he moved it from his 'to-do' list to his "got it done list". At the end of the week, instead of berating himself for still having things to do, he was able to appreciate all the tasks he had accomplished, which motivated him to continue the following week.

I have great systems in place in my business to ensure that everyone stays focused on their tasks but when they break down, it is down to me. Instead of drafting commercial documents or writing training courses, I put a headset on and start taking client phone calls. I am easily distracted. I love to talk to people and can often make myself late because I don't want to leave an interesting conversation with a stranger.

The system I use to create accountability is to schedule actions and to book meetings. In effect, I am making a public declaration, even if it is only to one other person, about what I will do and when. If I leave something festering on my to-do list, I know it will stay there forevermore unless I break it down into the actions required and schedule them into the day. The act of scheduling will make it clear when I am kidding myself. I can be wildly unrealistic about the things I can get done in the time available, but sometimes it can be the antidote to overwhelm – I realise that I *can* get everything done, with a little self-discipline and focus.

No one method works for everyone. It is important that you use the tools available to you to create account-ability and self-discipline and that you are self-aware enough to notice when you have veered off plan. This does not mean that you start again with a new plan; it is a feedback mechanism to flag when you might need to make an adjustment.

CASE STUDY: Abdul

Abdul is a senior commercial solicitor and a notary with twenty years of experience. He runs a good practice but is confident that there is room for improvement. He has an excellent legal secretary that deals with the administration for him but he is conscious that no one else in the team knows what she does. This means that his practice effectively pauses when she is on holiday. He begins a three-month accountability project with a notary that he knows in a different city, at a similar level to him. He wants to create a self-sufficient notarial department within his firm that can include another notary and another legal secretary. His plan is to pass most of the notary work to a more junior associate and oversee the department. He recognises that, as the most senior person in his firm, he will benefit from being held accountable by an independent notary who understands what he is aiming for.

Boundaries

I often speak about myself in the third person, I don't even realise that I am doing it. For example, before a client meeting, I warn people who are signing foreign language documents that 'the notary will have no sense of humour on this subject. She will ask you whether you understand the document and she will expect you to confirm that you do.' It's a bit of an odd habit but it helps me to create clean, firm boundaries with clients so that everyone understands what is expected and required of them.

For your first-class notarial practice to come into being, you must create space between yourself and your new systems to give your ideas a chance to work. For example, if you have devised clinic hours for your notarial work, mark these in your calendar and keep them sacrosanct. This means that your solicitor clients cannot see you during this time and you are not available for meetings or anything other than notary work. If you do not have clients booked in, use the time for notary training or one of the many other tasks that your notarial practice requires. As we discussed in the last chapter, your ideas will only become reality with action. An easy way to start is by dedicating specific time each week to your practice and enforcing this boundary.

As well as protecting your time you must conserve your energy. This means maintaining boundaries to safeguard your mental clarity, your physical health, your emotional wellbeing and your focus. This will require that you pick your battles. It is easy as a notary to be pulled into a position where you are doing the client's job for them, and usually for free. Before you know it, you are redrafting their documents, ringing their lawyer overseas to explain requirements or rearranging your whole day to accommodate their deadlines. This will not do for a first-class notary. You have systems in place in your notarial practice for good reason and you must allow them to work.

If you are not available because you are doing important solicitor work, you are not available. Just as you must protect your time for your notarial work, you must be equally dedicated and disciplined with your solicitor work. In reality, this is not as simple as it sounds, especially if you are the only notary available in your firm. Notaries can sometimes feel like the building's first aider and when a notarial client needs you, it can be difficult to say, 'Not now.' But this is what is required, if you are to build a first-class notarial practice, and this is why you are building systems to create structure and consistency. This applies equally to sole practitioners. If you want a notarial practice that is manageable and does not spill into every corner of your life, you have to create boundaries between yourself and your systems so that your practice runs like a well-oiled machine.

Training

As discussed earlier in the book, a first-class notarial practice needs a team of people in addition to the notary. It is not a solo project, even for sole practitioners. If you are currently doing everything yourself, you must build a team – this is the only way to create longevity and peace within your business. Every person who touches your notarial practice is part of your team. Solicitor-notaries, you need to train at least two assistants who can follow your phone script, take client details, open a matter and prepare a fee quote using your price list. This will take some effort upfront – you will need to sit down with your chosen staff and go through everything with them, but it will be worth it. Be realistic and schedule one training session a week for four consecutive weeks so that questions that arise during the week can be addressed.

The mistake that most notaries make is to only train one person and then become utterly reliant on that individual. This is not an effective system. You are building a practice that generates time-freedom, so do not fall into the trap of digging shallow foundations. If you are not yet senior within your solicitor practice, you may need to demonstrate to the decision-maker how you intend to build your notarial practice for the benefit of the firm to be allocated the resources required. If you are a sole practitioner notary without the resources yet for a full-time member of staff, be open minded about help available to you, such as a family member or virtual assistant.

Allow errors

Inevitably, errors will occur and that's OK. Repeatedly, you will think it would be easier to do it yourself and, during the training period, that is true. However, you are building a new kind of practice that is going to work brilliantly for you and your clients for many years to come. You are developing an amazing client conversion tool for your solicitor practice, or a solid and reliable practice that will create a wonderful income for you and your family. To do this, you must train staff to carry out notarial administration and accept that there will be some errors for at least the first couple of months, but once you see it up and running, it is enlightening.

When an error occurs, such as the wrong fee has been given or incorrect information collected, you need to remember that mistakes are all part of the system-building process. It will either be because the system has not been followed (human error) or the system has a gap or a flaw (system error). Identify which it is and fix it at your weekly training meeting. It will take a while to perfect the flow of your practice.

The key to a well-functioning team is having the right people doing the right roles. To build your team you have to let go of two limiting beliefs. The first is that you are the best person to do all roles. This is a difficult belief to disengage with because it is, for now at least, a true one. At this moment in time, you know more about every role within your notarial practice than anyone else and you can do every role better than anyone else. However, this does not mean that you are the *right* person for these roles going forward.

The second limiting belief, which may also be true currently, is that your practice is not busy enough or profitable enough to justify having a team to run it. However, you are building structural foundations to facilitate the growth of your practice. You cannot wait until the practice is busy to train the team. You need to have a degree of faith and build the practice infrastructure before it is needed. Perhaps you'll need a lot of faith, but this is always the case with a new department within a law firm. Until it is up and running and generating profit, you have to proceed on the basis that it will be successful.

Stand back

Once you have trained your team, you must stay in your own lane. Do not muddy the waters by interfering where you are not required. Your job is to make sure that the overall system works, which requires that everyone perform their allocated roles. This is not always easy. I am guilty of tinkering and tampering where I am not needed in a misguided effort to assist, but in truth, it's to alleviate boredom or do a job that is easier than the one I should be doing.

Summary

In trying to bring about your ideal notarial practice, discipline is crucial. You will never get *everything* done – and neither will I – but this should drive rather than undermine your efforts.

Your notarial practice department can be a shining beacon of efficiency and order, a happy little ship in a sea of long-standing open matters and work in progress.

Provided that you can be disciplined, you can quickly become the gold standard of client care and professional excellence. Notarial clients are generally happy and appreciative clients who give wonderful feedback. Make it your mission to be the five-star review department, and deliver on this by maintaining discipline in your notarial practice – making yourself accountable, setting and enforcing boundaries and training up a high-quality team as your priorities. With these tools at your disposal, just think how many of your goals you could achieve within a year.

ACTIONS

1. How do you intend to keep yourself accountable while you build your perfect notarial practice?

2. Do you feel that you have the correct boundaries in place to protect your solicitor work, your time and your peace of mind?

3. Which roles would make up your ideal notarial team?

4. What training plan would you need to implement to make your team highly effective?

5. Are you able and prepared to step back from some tasks and allow everyone in your team to fulfil their assigned roles?

TEN
Contribution

In a small legal profession with only around 800 practising members, everything you do matters. How you run your practice matters. All your actions as a notary are either contributing to the profession or detracting from it. There is no neutral. You may tell yourself that you are just one notary, practising at a low level in the northwest of England or on the outskirts of Cardiff, but as a first-class notary running an excellent practice, you have influence and impact, regardless of whether you recognise it.

How will you use your power? To contribute to the profession means that you are making it better. This is a subjective consideration. What do you believe would make our profession better? If you took the time to think about it, what improvements could you suggest, even if you don't know how they would be implemented? As a practising notary public, you are in the best position to suggest and assess ways in which our profession could be improved. What do you admire about it? What would you like to see more of? What do you think detracts from notarial practice and how could this be reduced or eliminated? You do not need to have a specific action plan for your contribution at this stage, but you must acknowledge that your opinions and actions matter.

Building a legacy

We are such a niche legal profession that every member counts. We need fresh thinkers. The notaries qualifying at the moment are exceptionally well trained and they need room to manoeuvre. They need to be welcomed into the profession because they are the ones who are going to take it into the next generation. We cannot afford to be defensive or protective about our incomes. If we do this, we are cutting off the oxygen to the entire profession and we will extinguish ourselves. The right attitude requires that you let go of the scarcity mindset and accept that the profession is ever evolving.

Although it is closely aligned with tradition and history, and at times can even appear somewhat old fashioned, the rules regarding hierarchy and status that might curtail you in another legal profession are less important in notarial practice. All notaries are equal. Some have a deeper skillset and others have more experience, but you can create a brilliant notarial practice and make a valuable contribution at one year or thirty years qualified. You just need to curate your perfect practice and implement your plan.

As an individual

The fact is, we are all going to retire at some point, so we need to have an elegant exit plan. The only way to retire graciously is to have something even better that you want to do. That way, you can hand over your notarial practice to the next notary and do so with enthusiasm. This is not always easy, I know, but it is something to work towards. Think of it as building a legacy. We cannot take it with us; we are going to leave it to someone, so build your practice with this in mind. What do you need to do now to hand over your practice with pride and a sense of achievement?

As a profession

As we discussed earlier in the book, our reputation as a profession is formed through each interaction that we have with every client and the way that we all run our individual practices. The standards that we hold ourselves to are the strands that weave the tapestry of the notarial profession. How we govern ourselves dictates the way that the profession evolves.

My father was fond of reminding each of his seven children that 'You are a Beckett,' the implication being that this carried with it a higher standard. You are a notary. As notaries, we are all responsible for the evolution of the profession. No one is exempt. This is true whether you are a scrivener notary in the City of London, a retired solicitor-notary working from home in rural Cornwall or a busy solicitor-notary in the centre of Manchester. We are all equally responsible for our professional legacy, and we must ensure that our contribution to the profession is the best that it can be.

CASE STUDY: Greg

Greg is a solicitor-notary in the north-west of England. He is an equity partner in his law firm and qualified as a notary five years ago. He enjoys his notarial practice but does not consider himself to have any real standing in the profession. He is confident that he is compliant but does not feel that he has sufficient experience to warrant a place on the Notaries Society Council or any sort of advisory committee. Greg would love to take his notarial practice to the next level but he feels he qualified too late in his career to have a meaningful impact.

The mistake Greg is making is that he is discounting his vast experience of running a law firm and ignoring his skill as a connector. He is also overlooking the advantage that his recent training gives him. The truth is, that Greg is in the perfect position to create a first-class notarial practice. He can create a network of notaries who are willing to assist and collaborate – in fact, he is still in touch with most of the notaries that he qualified with. He can put himself forward as a supervisor and register his interest in joining the Notaries Society Council. As a solicitor, he specialises in cyber security so he has incredibly useful skills, knowledge and experience that he can bring to the notarial profession if he is willing to make himself known.

Do not wait for permission to be a key player. Become conscious of your skillset and your advantages and put yourself forward for the positions that you want.

Be an ambassador

Every single notary public practising in England and Wales is an ambassador for the notarial profession. We are experts in this niche area of law and we must hold ourselves out as such. We are not glorified commissioners for oaths. Our duty in every case is to the transaction and we must take our responsibilities seriously. However, this does not mean that we need to dramatise our role or create unnecessary pomp and ceremony. We must be able to see the notarial interaction from the client's point of view and seek to build user-friendly practices.

As a first-class notary and an ambassador for the notarial profession, you should always be looking for ways to contribute to the profession. There are numerous ways in which you can do this.

Your standards

The first is in the way that you conduct yourself and the standards that you hold yourself to. This means that you must run the best possible practice that you can. It does not need to be the biggest practice or most well-known, but once you have created your ideal practice blueprint that works for you and works for your clients, you need to manage that practice in line with the highest standards.

Your practice should be a shining beacon of brilliance that encourages more people to qualify as notaries and enhances our reputation as international lawyers, both in the UK and overseas. Position yourself at the cutting edge of the legal sphere in whatever way you can, and remind yourself daily that you are an important ambassador for notarial practice. This should be reflected in your documents and in every interaction that you have.

Annual CPE is the minimum requirement and not the optimum level of training. This is just the level that the Faculty Office has assessed as the bare minimum. Don't let this be your standard. There are several courses that you can access and every module is designed to make you a better notary. Use all the brilliant resources available to you to become a first-class notary.

Help others

The second way that you can demonstrate your contribution to the profession is to teach, mentor, train and supervise. Even before you are eligible to act as a supervisor, you should take this responsibility seriously. Be helpful to your peers and have an attitude of inclusion. We are a collaborative profession and that is one of the things that makes us such a wonderful group. We all need help at one time or another. Even notaries with one year's PQE can be an invaluable source of support and professional friendship to newly qualified notaries. If you hear of another notary qualifying in your area, pick up the phone to introduce yourself and let them know that you're available as a friendly and helpful ear.

Ideally, you should have an enthusiastic and eager associate within your law firm who is keen to qualify and be part of the first-class practice that you are creating. When they qualify, you should be generous with your knowledge and your clients.

Spread the word

The third way that you can demonstrate your contribution is to educate your solicitor colleagues and contacts about the work that a notary does. We need more notaries to qualify, and as a first-class professional, you should be a fountain of encouragement and inspiration. You must be able and willing to convince your solicitor colleagues of the huge benefits of having a notarial department within the firm, and your notarial department should be the epitome of excellence and client conversion. Don't let our work go unacknowledged; what we do is valuable – someone should be shouting about it, and that someone can be you.

Go over and above

There are so many additional jobs that need doing for our profession to thrive. Pick something that suits you and enjoy it. You could become an inspector for the Faculty Office, or stand for election for the Notaries Society Council. If you are an IT expert, you could collaborate with the Notaries Society Council on the technological aspects of notarial practice. You could write articles for its quarterly publication. You might want to create a local notary network to meet once a quarter and discuss current matters and any new types of instructions that are coming through. What would you be most suited to?

Do no harm

As well as furthering the profession, you must take utmost care that you do not damage it. This is something that terrifies many notaries, myself included. We live in fear of a complaint being made against us to the Faculty Office or the Notaries Society, even when we are doing nothing wrong. A claim being made against a notary is extraordinarily rare, but we are still disproportionately worried about it happening. This is not a bad starting point and is better than the alternative maverick attitude of not caring. However, this fear needs to be kept in check if you are going to build a first-class practice.

You need to be able to recognise how you are impacting the profession currently. The antidote to excessive and unnecessary caution is to read all the Faculty Office rules and regulations. This will not take you long at all and will give you great confidence in running and growing your practice. When you know what you cannot do, you also know what you can do. If you then take the time to discuss your policies and procedures with other notaries, you will be reassured that you are doing things correctly, learn even better ways of working and become aware of anything you are currently doing that perhaps you shouldn't. This allows you to put it right.

Futureproofing

Our aim should be to hand over to the next generation of notaries a profession that is even better than the one that we joined. We are at a crucial turning point in the development of our profession. We need to move with the times and accept that our beloved hand press seals are likely to become a thing of the past. I recently had to show my twenty-three-year-old notarial assistant a chequebook and explain how they work. I have never felt so old. Like handwritten registers and protocols, our wafers and seals will be replaced by clever electronic versions and our seals will become ornaments that we dust now and then with fond nostalgia.

Rather than fear progress as something that will make us obsolete, we need to apply our brilliant minds to figuring out how we will be even more valuable in the next era of authentication. Rather than rage against the involvement of the Legal Services Board in the regulation of our profession, we need to position ourselves as the front runners of change. You may be thinking, 'How does this affect me personally and how can my practice influence this?' But this is your power as a member of the profession. You have influence. When you embrace change and you are willing to question things and speak up, you are altering the course of the profession, altering its trajectory.

Every year, the profession is evolving. We are ever so fond of our traditions and ceremonies but we must be proud also to be cutting-edge lawyers. As a solicitor-notary, your notarial practice should be a demonstration of excellence to your colleagues.

As solicitors, our progression tends to be mapped out for us. However, as notaries, we are required to actively create our progress within the profession. It can be tempting to stay in our own little spheres and let other people take on the roles of supervising, connecting, training and advising, but we are all responsible. We have a duty to our profession and we have a real and tangible influence. Next time you see a consultation paper email from the Faculty Office, open it, print it, read it and respond. It will take minutes, not hours, and you will be amazed at how valuable this is to the Faculty Office and, therefore, to our profession.

To share magnanimously, you need new and fresh ideas and you must know for certain that you have a first-class notarial practice that can generate more than enough work for all the people involved. This means that you have to play full out. You've got to be on the pitch and playing the game, not in the stands hoping not to be noticed. You must be visible, expert, efficient and bold.

Summary

Whatever your reason for qualifying as a notary public in England and Wales, you are now part of an illustrious club. You are in a privileged position of being able to make a difference in your profession. The way that the profession is regarded is a direct result of the actions and attitudes of its members.

You should be seeking to build a legacy, both as an individual notary and as a small part of a larger notarial legacy. You can do this by positioning yourself as an ambassador for the profession and making a contribution by upholding excellent standards for your own practice; helping others to enter and thrive in the profession; spreading the word about the excellent work being done by the profession and communicating its value to our solicitor colleagues; and going above and beyond, always looking for ways to contribute beyond your personal practice.

In realising your plan for your first-class notarial practice, always consider the bigger picture and consider how you can benefit the profession as a whole.

ACTIONS

Consider:

1. How could you contribute more to notarial practice in England and Wales?

2. Does your practice blueprint reflect the standards that you expect of the profession?

3. Do you feel open minded and optimistic about the changes that may affect the profession in the next five years?

4. Does your practice blueprint include your individual progression within the notarial profession?

5. If your practice was open to inspection by all new notaries, do you think that they would feel inspired and motivated? What would you improve?

Conclusion

Every year, around forty new notaries qualify in England and Wales and need to be welcomed into the profession. There is plenty of work for everyone and any notary can create a first-class practice, at any stage in their career. You may already have a brilliant business that you love and want to maintain for the next five, ten or twenty years. You may just need a few tweaks and adjustments to polish and perfect it. Perhaps you need to devise an exit plan or register your availability to supervise. You may be brand new and just starting in your notarial career and unsure of what is possible. Or you may want to redesign your notarial practice completely to create a new type of business or department that creates profit, time-freedom and career flexibility. Wherever you are currently, action is required.

Act now

If you feel overwhelmed by your notarial work and want to refine the instructions that you are dealing with – action is required. If you want to develop your practice to bring in more work – action is required. It does not take much to make big changes in a notarial practice, but action is what makes the difference. Action lists have been included at the end of each chapter of this book, and you may now have your own list of things that you could do, should do and fully intend to get around to. Don't overcomplicate it and don't procrastinate. When I speak to notaries who feel stuck in their current practice, in the vast majority of cases the missing ingredient is action. You must make space for business development in your schedule each week and keep this commitment to yourself sacred. If nothing changes then nothing will change.

If you take one thing away from this book, let it be that you can and must make a brilliant plan to transform and regenerate your notarial practice. I want you to be excited, exhilarated and optimistic about your qualifications and your potential. I will be thrilled to hear that you have moved up a fee bracket when you apply for your practising certificate if this is what you want. I will be equally excited to hear that you get to walk your children to school each morning without checking your phone. I will be delighted to learn what you have achieved or to receive a photo of you enjoying a glass of champagne on your dream holiday that you paid for using the additional income you've generated.

We all bring better service to clients when we are running happy, efficient and expert practices. We strengthen and bolster the profession when we collaborate with our governing body and with each other. Commit to becoming a first-class notary and running an even better practice every year.

Your blueprint

Now that you've finished the book, take out your practice blueprint once again and look at it with fresh eyes. Identify the actions that you think would yield the best return on investment. Some people like to take the most challenging action and get it out of the way. Others prefer to create momentum by tackling the easiest things first. I like to prioritise by assessing what will create the most time, money or both.

Consider whether your ideal practice is aspirational and motivating. Does it excite and inspire you? If not, go back and make it better. Make it *exactly* what you want. To build a first-class notarial practice you must love your business and get a buzz out of it. I want every notary enquiry to give you a lift in your day and be welcome to you because it is a building block for your ideal practice. It is easy to become fatigued with a notary practice because the work can be repetitive and, without a plan that you are working towards, it can feel like treading water. So make it fun. If you want a new iPad, a sports car or a posh pen, write it into your plan. Or you might want to choose a charity that you can support with a monthly donation. Make your practice blueprint a document that you want to pull out every Monday morning.

You know the actions required to take you from where you are with your notarial practice to where you want to be. Your mission is to be visible, expert, efficient and bold. I wish you the best of luck with your notarial practice. I hope that you make brilliant choices and create a wonderful practice that serves clients ethically and professionally. I trust that you will act for the good of our profession and that we will continue to be the oldest legal profession in the United Kingdom for many years to come.

Acknowledgements

I would like to thank my notarial colleagues at The Notary Solution, who make running this business such a pleasure: Alex Smith, Nick Dyson, Adam Wood, Annaliese Barber, Ann-Marie Lee, Gayle Mellard and Emma Ladd.

Thank you also to Sharif Ela, Lindsay Sharp, Stephen Gordon, Howard Dellar, Ann-Marie Lee, Emma Ladd and Annaliese Barber for reading the draft manuscript and giving me valuable feedback.

Thank you to the fantastic team at Rethink Press for the detailed guidance and expertise, particularly Lucy McCarraher, Kerry Boettcher and Anke Ueberberg.

Special thanks go to my lovely husband John Benson, for his endless patience and support through this book-writing process, and to my business partner, sister and wonderful friend, Fran Foley, for keeping me sane, organised, grounded and profitable.

The Author

Katherine Beckett is a notary public based in Harrogate, North Yorkshire and founder and director of The Notary Solution, a multi-notary practice. She qualified as a solicitor in 2003 and notary public in 2004. She has been elected to the Council of the Notaries Society of England and Wales and has supervised several newly qualified notaries. She has also written and delivered Faculty Office-accredited training to notaries throughout England and Wales since 2010.

Find out more about Katherine's services at:

- 🌐 www.thenotarysolution.co.uk
- ✉ Katherine.beckett@thenotarysolution.co.uk
- f www.facebook.com/TheNotarySolution
- in www.linkedin.com/company/
  the-notary-solution-limited

www.ingramcontent.com/pod-product-compliance
Lightning Source LLC
Chambersburg PA
CBHW011301210326
41599CB00037B/7109